CREATIVE RESOURCES FOR YOUTH MINISTRY

Creative Communication and Discussion Activities

CREATIVE RESOURCES FOR YOUTH MINISTRY

Creative Communication and Discussion Activities

Compiled by Wayne Rice and Mike Yaconelli
Edited by Yvette Nelson

Saint Mary's Press
Christian Brothers Publications
Winona, Minnesota

The contents of this book are reprinted with permission from *Tension Getters, Tension Getters Two,* and *Amazing Tension Getters,* published by Youth Specialties (Grand Rapids, MI: Zondervan Publishing House, 1981, 1985, 1988).

The publishing team for this book included Robert P. Stamschror, development editor; Mary Duerson Kraemer, copy editor; Maura C. Goessling, production editor; David Piro, cover designer; pre-press, printing, and binding by the graphics division of Saint Mary's Press.

Printed in the United States of America

Printing: 8 7 6 5 4 3

Year: 1998 97

ISBN 0-88489-266-2

Contents

Introduction

Youth Ministry Today   *9*
Creative Strategies   *11*

Case Study Method   *12*
Notes   *13*

Part 1: Making a Choice

Introduction   *15*
Caught in the Middle 1   *16*
Caught in the Middle 2   *16*
Caught in the Middle 3   *16*
Taking a Position 1   *16*
Taking a Position 2   *17*
Taking a Position 3   *17*
It Is Your Job 1   *17*
It Is Your Job 2   *17*
It Is Your Job 3   *17*
Honest, I Didn't Do It   *18*
Honest, Mom, I Didn't Do It   *18*
Honest, Dad, I Didn't Do It   *18*
Take a Hard Look 1   *19*
Take a Hard Look 2   *19*
Take a Hard Look 3   *19*
Winners and Losers 1   *19*
Winners and Losers 2   *20*
Winners and Losers 3   *20*
Who Is Right? 1   *21*
Who Is Right? 2   *21*
Who Is Right? 3   *21*
Maybe Yes, Maybe No? 1   *21*
Maybe Yes, Maybe No? 2   *22*
Maybe Yes, Maybe No? 3   *22*
It Is Your Decision 1   *22*
It Is Your Decision 2   *22*
It Is Your Decision 3   *23*

Changing Places 1   *23*
Changing Places 2   *23*
Changing Places 3   *23*
How Do You Spell Equal? 1   *24*
How Do You Spell Equal? 2   *24*
How Do You Spell Equal? 3   *24*
To Die or Not to Die 1   *25*
To Die or Not to Die 2   *25*
To Die or Not to Die 3   *25*
In the Eye of the Beholder   *26*
If You Do, I Will   *26*
Yes You May; No You Won't   *26*
The Disappearing Failure
   Notice   *27*
Caught in the Middle   *27*
The Stepfather Dilemma   *27*
Why Me?   *27*
Stretching the Truth   *28*
What He Doesn't Know Won't
   Hurt Him   *28*
No Big Deal   *28*
Bart and the Bottle   *28*
Did They or Didn't They?   *29*
See No Evil, Speak No Evil   *29*
Truth in Lending   *29*
Who Will Listen?   *29*
Read It or Watch It   *30*
Saving Money   *30*

One-track Mind *30*
Saving Face or Losing It *30*
Two Dates in One *31*
The Sex Talk *31*
To Tell or Not to Tell *31*
Getting Even *32*
A Hungry Situation *32*
It Is a Long Walk Home *32*
Working Hard or Hardly
    Working *32*
There Goes the
    Neighborhood *33*
Are You Prejudiced? *33*
He Works Hard for His
    Money *34*
Kicking and Screaming *34*
Eye for an Eye *34*

The Flat Tire *35*
It Runs in the Family *35*
A Tough Decision *36*
Sweet Sixteen *36*
The Conflict *36*
No One Will Ever Know *37*
Forgetful *37*
Special-Order Baby *37*
A Friendly Lunch *38*
The Playmate Locker *38*
Do Me a Favor *39*
Whose Life Do You Support? *39*
On the Outside Looking In *40*
Heartthrob *40*
Teenage Mom *41*
Soaps and Sex *41*

Part 2: Forming an Opinion ━━━━━

Introduction *43*
This Can't Be Happening *44*
Change of Mind *44*
Be True to Your Friends *44*
Never Admit More Than They
    Know *45*
Mellow Fellow *46*
What's Important? *46*
Nuclear Pie *46*
Negative Outlook *47*
It Is My Body *47*
I Don't Want to Die *48*
Don't Knock Rock *48*
Sex Is for Everyone *48*
After Sex, Then What? *49*
Picky Parents *49*
School Is No Big Deal *50*
Phony Kids *50*
Old-fashioned *51*
The Beautiful People *51*

Immoral Majority *52*
Just Waiting *52*
No Difference *53*
Confidentiality *53*
Driving While Intoxicated *53*
Under Control *53*
Hunger Hurts *54*
Home, Sweet Home *54*
What Is Justice? *54*
Boycott *55*
Sex, Drugs, and Rock 'n' Roll *55*
There Has to Be a Better Way *55*
Who Can You Turn To? *56*
Waiting *56*
The Rip-off *56*
Party Time *57*
A School Night's Secret
    Meeting *57*
God and Rock 'n' Roll *57*
A Disturbing Issue *58*

Part 3: Ranking Actions and Decisions

Introduction *59*

Be Home by Ten *60*

It Won't Happen to Me *60*

Double Trouble *61*

Only This Once *62*

Keep It to Yourself *63*

Fight for Your Rights *63*

Is Marriage Forever? *64*

Is It Worth It? *64*

The Forgotten Birthday *65*

Making Ends Meet *66*

Who Cares? *66*

The Food Store Robbery *67*

The Party and the Practical
Joke *68*

The Two-timer *68*

It Happened So Fast *69*

Hard Choices *70*

The Last to Know *71*

No Place to Go *72*

Stepwitch *73*

The Dud Youth Worker *73*

Nobody Will Know *74*

The Double Cross *75*

Double Date—Double Trouble *76*

Little Things Mean a Lot *77*

The Champagne Dinner *78*

The Senior Prom *78*

Who Killed Raoul? *79*

Choosing Between Mom and
Dad *80*

A Gift or a Curse? *81*

Like Mother, Like Daughter *81*

Close Call *82*

The Search *83*

Less Than Perfect *84*

Partying *85*

X-Rated *85*

The Diary *86*

Secret Birth Control *86*

The End of a Future *87*

The Quitter? *88*

Fatso *88*

The Adulterer *89*

Part 4: Giving Advice

Introduction *91*

Violent Dilemma *92*

Christmas in Hawaii *92*

Big Sister, Big Problem *92*

Family Ties *92*

Would God Play the Lottery? *93*

Older Man, Younger Woman *93*

Who to Tell? *94*

Good Friend to a Bad Friend *94*

The Boy Who Wouldn't Give
Up *94*

Little Sister *95*

The Wrong Curves *95*

The Loner *96*

Introduction

Youth Ministry Today: Its Growth and Development

For the past twenty years, Catholic youth ministry has been in the process of critically re-examining its philosophy, goals, and principles. In part, this re-examination grew out of the perceived and felt needs of young people who will be the adults of the twenty-first century. In the early seventies—before youth ministry, as we know it, existed—those who worked with young people saw a need to experiment with new styles and forms of ministry with young people. Many parishes, schools, and dioceses began to develop youth ministries on the solid foundation of relational ministry and on the unique social and developmental needs of young people. Heretofore they had relied on the unquestioned process of presenting organizational, programmatic approaches such as weekly or biweekly classes, sports programs, or rarely, weekend or overnight retreats.

The new processes and approaches planted and tended during those years produced a renewed ministry with young people based on experience and insight. Leaders in the field of youth ministry discovered that ministry with young people must be a multifaceted, comprehensive, and coordinated effort. They rediscovered the age-old truth of Jesus' ministry: all ministry is rooted in relationships. Through the leaders' outreach and relationship building, young people began to experience the warmth of an accepting community, which is vital for the development of a comprehensive youth ministry. As relationships grew, a sense of belonging and participation also grew. The experience of acceptance, belonging, and participation opened young people so that they were able to reveal the needs and the concerns that preoccupied them. Programs developed around these needs and concerns: service projects, retreats, new forms of catechesis, peer ministry, prayer groups, celebrations of the sacraments. With these rediscovered opportunities for ministry, youth ministers were in a position to help young people grow personally and spiritually and find their place in the faith community as active Catholic Christians with a mission.

As the style of youth ministry changed, the traditional ministry to young people by the community evolved into a fourfold approach. Youth ministry was conceived not only in terms of responding *to* the unique social and developmental needs of young people but also in terms of adults' sharing a common ministry *with* young people, *by* young people (especially involving their peers), and *for* young people (adults interpreting young people's legitimate concerns and acting as advocates for them). This fourfold understanding—to, with, by, and for—changed the style and broadened the scope of youth ministry.

In 1975 and 1976, hundreds of youth leaders from across the country consulted for fifteen months and concretized the aims and philosophy of youth ministry in a document called *A Vision of Youth Ministry.* It has served to guide the church's mission to young people ever since. *A Vision of Youth Ministry* affirmed the growth that had taken place in youth ministry and challenged the whole church to renew itself.

The document clearly places youth ministry within the framework of the mission and ministry of the church. It defines youth ministry as the "response of the Christian community to the needs of young people, and the sharing of the unique gifts of youth with the larger community."[1] This reciprocal relationship helps the community to view youth ministry as part of the entire ministry of the community, not separate from it—a problem often encountered when a ministry with young people is perceived as a club or an organization set apart from the mainstream of church life. *A Vision of Youth Ministry* makes clear that an effective ministry with young people incorporates them into the life of the community, where they can share their gifts and talents with the whole community. If young people are to have positive experiences of church life, they must have opportunities to be involved in the whole life of the community. Such opportunities for this type of interaction are at the heart of youth ministry, not on the periphery. By being involved in church life with adults, young people gain a view of what it means to be an adult Catholic Christian. This is a special gift of adults to young people.

The categories of youth ministry as outlined in *A Vision of Youth Ministry* closely parallel the fundamental ministries of the church: word, worship and celebrating, creating community, and service and healing.[2] The seven categories of youth ministry describe the forms that this ministry should take. It is a common framework for a holistic ministry with young people. Briefly, the seven components of youth ministry are as follows:[3]

Word: proclaiming the Good News that leads young people to faith in Jesus (evangelization) and deepening young people's faith in Jesus and applying that faith to their everyday life (catechesis)

Worship: celebrating relationships in community and with the Lord through a variety of worship experiences, personal prayer, and spiritual development

Creating community: building relationships with young people and creating a healthy environment for growth, in which young people can experience acceptance, belonging, and participation

Guidance and healing: responding to young people's need for spiritual, moral, and personal counseling; vocational guidance; and reconciliation with self, others (peers and family), and God

Justice and service: educating young people to the demands of justice and the social problems of our world, responding to young people who suffer injustice, and motivating young people for service on behalf of others

Enablement: calling forth adults and young people to become ministers and providing them with the understanding and skills needed for effective ministry

Advocacy: working on behalf of young people, interpreting their concerns and needs, and standing up for them in the Christian, and larger, community

Youth ministry has experienced a renewal within the U.S. Catholic church. A renewed ministry with young people brings a need for new and better resources to assist leaders. Before turning to the resources found in this book, let's examine the place of creative social and learning strategies within youth ministry.

Creative Strategies for Youth Ministry

We have already seen the primacy of relationships in youth ministry. However, as relationships grow and programs are created, strategies are needed to accomplish youth ministry's tasks. The strategies in this book are aids. Their aim is to provide you with a variety of activities you can use in any number of programs. Some of these strategies are primarily suited for one or another component of youth ministry. However, most are adaptable to any number of components. All these strategies foster a particular type of learning—experiential learning. To understand its contribution to your youth ministry, let's examine experiential learning.

Experiential Learning

We have often heard it said that we learn from experience. This is true to an extent. But so much of our own life experience goes by without our ever learning from it. If young people's life experiences are to be sources of learning and growth, then young people must reflect upon and assimilate them. This often goes undone because no one takes time to help them reflect upon and learn from those experiences. In addition to life experience, there is a second source of experiential learning: structured experience. Experiences we develop that engage young people in the learning process and enable them to reflect are a rich resource for learning.

The structured experiences found in the Creative Resources series—communication games, learning strategies, simulations, projects, case studies, planning ideas, crowd-breakers, mixers, games, special events, and skits—are potential learning experiences for young people.

Case Study Method

Catholic social thought and Catholic moral theology aim to sustain and support the fullness of human life. Catholic social thought does not view the human community as a necessary evil that compels individuals to put up with people they would rather not be with. Rather, Catholic social thought sees human beings as *essentially* related, as people who are at their best when they are in community, when they are *with and for* one another. Throughout two thousand years of life and reflection, the church has developed a uniquely Catholic perspective, one that sometimes agrees with and sometimes finds itself at odds with the prevailing value system.

Individual Catholics are able to draw on this body of Catholic thought and this embodied Catholic way of being. Catholics can draw support from the faith of the church, whose moral guidelines are based on the Commandments, the Beatitudes, and those gospel values held and lived and reflected on throughout its long tradition. Individual Catholics are also able to draw on papal documents and bishops' pastorals that, in times of great risk and uncertainty, call our attention to the issues of life itself, of war and peace, and of economic justice, to name a few.

It is your task and privilege as a youth leader to help young people arrive at solutions that express and integrate Catholic values. These solutions may require you to present values that the young people, as a matter of fact, do not hold or are having a difficult time understanding or accepting. These values need not be "laid on" young people, but they must be presented as part of their Catholic heritage. Guided by the Scriptures, the church's Tradition, and the prevailing sense of the faithful, individuals are better able to make their own decision following their informed conscience in a given set of particular circumstances.

Case studies provide you and the young people an occasion to reason, reflect, and pray together. From the starting point of a hypothetical but real-life situation, the case method challenges participants to discuss the various options and to develop and hone skills in decision-making. The case study becomes a springboard for discussion and for the involvement of participants by raising questions to which they may develop alternative answers rather than receiving clear-cut solutions, which are in any case usually difficult to arrive at. (Those situations that do in fact have clear-cut solutions make for brief discussions and short sessions.) The situations here are designedly thorny and do not admit of easy answers, but they do ask of the young people careful and prayerful thought, engagement, and an acknowledgment and assessment of their own values. The case studies allow those involved to develop analytic skills and to apply principles that support their decisions. The following general considerations will help you effectively use the case-study method:

1. Offer the participants a chance to ask questions about the purpose and the process involved in the case study.
2. Encourage careful listening among the participants.

3. Explore the difference between subjective and objective opinions.
4. Encourage the participants to respect one another's opinions.
5. Keep the group on task; avoid tangents that tend to confuse the issue.
6. Stress that all information given is important and worthy of consideration.
7. If necessary, offer time for the participants to study resource material that can help them reach a solution.
8. If necessary, build in follow-up time.
9. Be creative; feel free to modify the process to accommodate your needs and situation.

Notes

1. United States Catholic Conference (USCC), *A Vision of Youth Ministry* (Washington, DC: USCC, Department of Education, 1976), p. 4.

2. For a contemporary description of the fundamental ministries of the church, see James Dunning, "About Ministry: Sharing Our Gifts," *PACE* 8 (1977) and *PACE* 9 (1978).

3. USCC, *A Vision of Youth Ministry,* p. 7.

PART 1

Making a Choice

Introduction

Most of the case studies in this section ask the young people to discuss what they *would* do and then what they *should* do. The first part of the discussion requires honesty, and the second, clarity. Young people are willing to be honest when they find themselves in a welcoming, accepting setting. They need to feel free to speak the views they deeply hold about each situation. They need to be able to expect that their views will be received and respected.

The second step requires the pooling, presentation, and defense of the values behind each decision put forward by the young people. At this point, you as youth minister are in a position to present, if necessary, the broader moral considerations grounded in the Gospel and mediated, held, and shared by the church.

Caught in the Middle 1

Carla is a teacher's aide for English class. The teacher has entrusted her with the job of taking attendance each day as soon as class begins. Before class, a guy that Carla has been wanting to date asks her to mark him present even though he is going to cut the class. He quickly walks away before Carla can give an answer.

- What would you do in Carla's situation? Why?
- What should you do in Carla's situation? Why?

Caught in the Middle 2

Some of your friends invite you to go with them to the movies tonight. It sounds like you will have a good time if you go. When you arrive at the movies, you realize that your friends have decided to sneak into the theater through a side door. You have to think quickly. Should you sneak in with your friends, pay for your ticket and sit with your friends even though they did not pay, or walk home?

- What would you do? Why?
- What should you do? Why?

Caught in the Middle 3

Your English class has gone to the library to work on a research assignment. Several of your friends are goofing around while you are trying to work. One of your friends pulls the fire alarm. The librarian blames you, and you are suspended from school for a day. You don't want to squeal on your friend, but you don't really want to be suspended either.

- What would you do? Why?
- What should you do? Why?

Taking a Position 1

Mary found out yesterday that she is pregnant. She knows her parents will never forgive her. Recently, a neighbor's daughter became pregnant, and when Mary's father heard about it, he said that the girl should be kicked out of the house. Mary is afraid her dad will do something like that if he finds out about her pregnancy. In desperation, Mary turns to you. She has made up her mind to get an abortion, but she wants your opinion first. She is not sure if abortion is right or wrong, but it seems to be the only logical solution to her situation.

- What would you do? Why?
- What should you do? Why?

Taking a Position 2

You just found out that a student in one of your classes is a homosexual. On the way home from school, he sits next to you on the bus and asks you what you think about homosexuality.

■ What would you do? Why?
■ What should you do? Why?

Taking a Position 3

You keep hearing these opinions about sex from students in your health class at school: Sex is something to be enjoyed. Everyone is doing it. Sex is a personal choice. If you love the person, then sex is all right. After class, the student sitting next to you asks for your opinion. The student knows that you are a Catholic.

■ What would you do? Why?
■ What should you do? Why?

It Is Your Job 1

It is Friday afternoon. You have to be at work in one hour. You have just gotten off the phone with a friend who invited you to a party tonight. You have been grounded for the last two weeks. This is your first free night, but you have to work. You decide to call in sick and go to the party. The next day at work, your boss asks you how you are feeling.

■ What would you do? Why?
■ What should you do? Why?

It Is Your Job 2

You work at an ice-cream parlor. This is your first real job; you work after school three days per week. You have noticed that the other employees, who are all about your age, give free ice cream to their friends. When three of your friends visit the store one afternoon and ask for a free scoop of ice cream, you decide that it is all right to give them one.

One day, the boss leaves you in charge of the store. You see one of the other employees giving away ice cream to a friend. When you tell him not to give free ice cream, he says, "You do it, why can't I?"

■ What would you do? Why?
■ What should you do? Why?

It Is Your Job 3

You have been working part-time at a record store for six months, and you are still not making minimum wage. You have tried to get another job, but you have had no luck. You took this job to make some extra spending money, but after you pay for gas and insurance on your car, you have very little left.

One day, the boss asks you to mark down the prices on some of the older tapes for an upcoming sale. A friend of yours, who also works at the store, says you should mark down some of the new tapes. That way the two of you could afford to buy the new ones. He reasons that your boss is not even paying you minimum wage, so you deserve the opportunity to buy at a discount.

- What would you do? Why?
- What should you do? Why?

Honest, I Didn't Do It

Three weeks ago you wrecked your parents' car. This is the first time since the accident that your parents have allowed you to use the car. As you are parking in the school parking lot, you hit a pole. Your parents told you before you left for the football game that if you had another accident, they would take away your license. You consider telling them that somebody hit you in the parking lot. You know that they would believe the story and that you would keep your driver's license.

- What would you do? Why?
- What should you do? Why?

Honest, Mom, I Didn't Do It

Your parents are gone for the weekend. They left you at home to watch the house. You are the only one there. Before they left, your parents told you that you can go out with your friends but you are not to have anyone over to the house while they are gone. A friend of yours talks you into throwing a small party. You decide that your parents will never find out. During the party, someone breaks your mother's favorite vase. You try to glue it back together, but you cannot. When your parents return, you tell them the dog broke the vase.

Later in the week, a neighbor mentions to your mother that she thought you had a few friends at the house over the weekend. Your mother asks you if anyone was at the house while she and your father were gone.

- What would you do? Why?
- What should you do? Why?

Honest, Dad, I Didn't Do It

It is Friday night. Sharon's boyfriend has invited her to his house for pizza and television. When she arrives, Sharon finds that her boyfriend's parents are not home and will not be home until late in the evening. Sharon's parents have told her not to be at her boyfriend's home when his parents are not there. She decides to stay anyway, knowing that her parents will never find out. When she gets home that evening, Sharon's dad asks how her boyfriend's parents are doing.

- What would you do in Sharon's situation? Why?
- What should you do in Sharon's situation? Why?

Take a Hard Look 1

Mary and Bill, two friends of yours, have decided to get an apartment together as soon as they graduate from school. They believe it is better for them to live together rather than to get married right away. They argue that their parents are divorced and that they don't want the same thing to happen to their relationship. Mary and Bill believe that living together will be a good way to test their relationship and that if things work out, they will marry in a few years. Bill and Mary value your opinion and want to know what you think.

- What would you do? Why?
- What should you do? Why?

Take a Hard Look 2

Peter has been struggling with his beliefs concerning sex. It seems that everyone at school thinks it is all right. Peter is not sure what the Bible says. He knows that sex outside of marriage is definitely wrong, but there is a lot that neither the church nor the Bible covers. That is what is bothering him. On his last date, Peter feels that he went too far. He is feeling guilty, but he is not sure what to do.

- What would you do in Peter's situation? Why?
- What should you do in Peter's situation? Why?

Take a Hard Look 3

Your dad thinks that you date the wrong type of people—at least that is what he tells you every chance he gets. He believes that you should only date Catholics, and that if there are none to date, you should just be content to wait. A friend of yours at church dates people who are not Catholic and sees nothing wrong with it. At the moment, you are not dating anyone. You want to date the right kind of person.

- What would you do? Why?
- What should you do? Why?

Winners and Losers 1

Today one more person must be cut from the basketball team. Ron, Chris, or Jim will probably be one of the players to be cut. All of them have equal ability. Ron and Chris are best friends and have decided to stick together and help each other out. They don't know Jim, and they see no reason to allow him to be chosen over either of them. They agree to make each other look better to the coach than Jim looks. During an afternoon scrimmage, Ron passes to Chris even when Jim is open for a shot. When Ron does pass to Jim, he bounces the basketball off Jim's knees, making him look uncoordinated. In the last seconds of the game, Jim is open for a shot, but Chris drives toward the basket, gets lucky, and scores.

At the end of practice, the coach cuts Jim from the team and congratulates Ron and Chris for their outstanding performances. Ron and Chris think that they did the right thing. Making the team was important, they reasoned, and they did what they had to do.

■ What would you have done in Chris and Ron's situation? Why?
■ What should you have done in Chris and Ron's situation? Why?

Winners and Losers 2

This is the toughest English class that Mary has ever taken. Since the class is required for graduation, Mary must pass it. The teacher grades on a strict curve. When tests are given, the teacher often leaves the room. The class takes advantage of the teacher's absence and cheats. Mary has considered telling the teacher, but she realizes that it would do no good. With everyone always cheating on tests, the curve is higher, making it harder for those not cheating to pass the class. Even though it is wrong, Mary considers cheating just enough to pass the class.

■ What would you do in Mary's situation? Why?
■ What should you do in Mary's situation? Why?

Winners and Losers 3

Bobby knows that no one ever talks to him because he is a loser. He has never been exceptional in sports, his weight has always been a problem, and his acne makes him look like he has the chicken pox. Jimmy, one of the most popular guys at school, talks to Bobby at church on Sunday, but on Monday morning, he acts as if Bobby does not exist. When Bobby and Jimmy pass in the halls, Bobby is ignored—especially when Jimmy is with his friends. Jimmy says it is tough being friends with Bobby at school because a person can't be a winner if he talks to losers. Jimmy thinks popularity is important and won't risk being friends with Bobby. Jimmy thinks he will lose his popularity if he talks to Bobby.

■ What would you do in Bobby's situation? Why?
■ What should you do in Bobby's situation? Why?

Who Is Right? 1

Your father has been having problems with his business. Creditors are calling every day to speak to him. He seems so depressed. He is talking about filing for bankruptcy. You wish that you could do something to help.

When the phone rings, you answer and the caller asks to speak to your father. Your father, who is standing nearby, tells you to say that he is not home.

- What would you do? Why?
- What should you do? Why?

Who Is Right? 2

Tom can't understand why his girlfriend, Sherri, is not allowed to go to parties. Her parents believe the only parties Sherri should attend are parties that are sponsored by the church. On Saturday night, when Tom and Sherri are invited to a party for a mutual friend, Sherri decides to go with Tom. She tells her parents that they are going to a movie. Tom and Sherri attend the party, have a great time, and Sherri makes certain that she is home on time. The next day in church, Sherri is with her father when he asks Tom what he thought of the movie.

- What would you do in Sherri's situation? Why?
- What should you do in Sherri's situation? Why?

Who Is Right? 3

Your parents forbid you to associate with Jerry. Ever since Jerry was busted at school for using drugs, your mother has been on your back to find another close friend, so you promised not to hang around with Jerry.

Friday night after the football game, you go to the local pizza place with some friends, and Jerry tags along. You see your parents sitting in the back of the restaurant. You don't think they see you, but you are not sure.

- What would you do? Why?
- What should you do? Why?

Maybe Yes, Maybe No? 1

It is Monday morning, and Jim has English class first period. Today is the only day the teacher will accept book reports. Jim knows he should have done his report. He needs an *A* in this class to qualify for a scholarship to a local college. If he does not hand in a report today, there is no way he can get an *A* in English. Jim remembers reading a review of a book in a magazine. He thinks about copying it and turning it in as his report. His older brother has also given him a report which received an *A* in the previous year's class. Jim thinks the teacher would never recognize the paper as being his brother's.

- What would you do in Jim's situation? Why?
- What should you do in Jim's situation? Why?

Maybe Yes, Maybe No? 2

The teacher instructs the students to exchange papers with the student next to them for grading. Every time the students do this, a lot of them "forget" to mark some of the answers wrong. The teacher works on the honor system and grades are reported orally, so he cannot tell if anyone cheats. You know that the person grading your paper cheats for you. Today he has asked you to cheat for him because he did not have much time to study last night. Because everyone cheats and the assignment was only homework, he believes that it is all right to ask you to skip over a few wrong answers.

- What would you do? Why?
- What should you do? Why?

Maybe Yes, Maybe No? 3

Your math teacher has left the class to handle an emergency. The grade book is being passed around the class. Because the teacher enters homework, quiz, and test grades in pencil, it is easy to change them. The grade book is getting close to you.

- What would you do? Why?
- What should you do? Why?

It Is Your Decision 1

Have you ever used drugs? That question jumps out at you from the application. You abused drugs in the past but not anymore. You know that if you answer no, you will be lying, but if you answer yes, you will undoubtedly lose your chance of getting the job. This is the only job you have a reasonable chance of getting. Good jobs have been tough to find in your community, and you desperately need this one.

- What would you do? Why?
- What should you do? Why?

It Is Your Decision 2

After a Friday night football game at your school, a few of your friends invite you to go out drinking beer at a neighborhood park. You decide to go. A friend of your parents drives by the park and sees you drinking. You think she will tell your parents what she saw, but you are not sure. Even though your parents drink, they disapprove of your doing so. As you are driving home from the park, you cannot decide whether to tell your parents you have been drinking or to wait and see if they confront you.

- What would you do? Why?
- What should you do? Why?

It Is Your Decision 3

A friend whose parents have left for the weekend is throwing a party. There must be at least fifty people in her living room. You and your friend Chris are having a great time talking to your friends and listening to music. Some people begin smoking marijuana. You want to leave, but Chris says there is no reason to because you are not the ones smoking.

- What would you do? Why?
- What should you do? Why?

Changing Places 1

Maria likes Carlos and she knows that Carlos likes her—she can tell by the way he looks at her in history class. However, Carlos is shy. He is afraid to ask Maria to go out with him because he thinks that she will say no. Carlos told his best friend that he likes Maria. His best friend told Maria about Carlos's feelings for her. Maria is confused.

- What would you do in Maria's situation? Why?
- What should you do in Maria's situation? Why?

Changing Places 2

Kimberly's name is on the front page of the school newspaper because she wants to try out for the school football team. At the lockers, in the cafeteria, and in the classrooms, people are questioning Kimberly's choice. Kimberly thinks she could make the team, but she isn't sure whether it is something a girl should be doing.

- What would you do in Kimberly's situation? Why?
- What should you do in Kimberly's situation? Why?

Changing Places 3

Mary Anne's grandparents have told her there is man's work and there is woman's work. They say a man should be the provider, and a woman should play the role of homemaker and mother. Mary Anne is graduating soon and is trying to decide what to do with her life. Her boyfriend, who is a premed student at a local university, wants to marry in a few years and start a family. Mary Anne has considered a career as an engineer, which for her would mean delaying marriage and possibly deciding not to have children.

■ What would you do in Mary Anne's situation? Why?
■ What should you do in Mary Anne's situation? Why?

How Do You Spell Equal? 1

Tracy's family thinks that Ron is a fine boy. However, her parents forbid her to date him because he is Korean. He was adopted when he was six months old. Ron has grown up in a typical suburban church where almost all the members are white. The church had accepted him until he wanted to date Tracy. Tracy's dad is on the church board. Everyone is talking. Tracy's parents are considering leaving the church. No matter what they do, Tracy's parents say their daughter is not going to date a Korean or any other minority person. They add that it is fine for Ron to participate in the church, and they are glad he is a Christian. However, they hold that his dating their daughter is a totally different matter.

■ What would you do in Ron's situation? Why?
■ What should you do in Ron's situation? Why?

How Do You Spell Equal? 2

The Group for Equality for All Ages is suing the Restaurant Association for giving a 10 percent discount to all senior citizens on dinners purchased at its member restaurants. The judge has heard both sides of the case and has to come to a decision.

■ What would you do in the judge's situation? Why?
■ What should you do in the judge's situation? Why?

How Do You Spell Equal? 3

Ambrose did not get the promotion he had been hoping for. He had been working for the city water department for nine years. His wife is pregnant with their second baby, and they need the additional money the promotion would have offered. An African-American woman with fewer qualifications than Ambrose received the promotion. It is all part of the city's equality program. Ambrose thinks that it is unfair because he deserved the promotion and worked hard to get it. He argues that it isn't his fault that the city had not hired enough minorities in the past. He says he is not prejudiced. He wonders why he should pay for past discriminatory hiring practices. He decides to sue the city.

■ What would you have done in Ambrose's situation? Why?
■ What should you have done in Ambrose's situation? Why?

To Die or Not to Die 1

Annie is a severely retarded nineteen-year-old. She has control of her motor (muscular) faculties, but seems to function at a chronological age of about one or two. Through nearly eight years of therapy, doctors and aids have taught her to button the buttons on her clothes. Annie seems unable to learn even the simplest tasks that would enable her to hold an extremely simple job on a factory production line.

Providing for Annie's care will take large expenditures by taxpayers and Annie's family. In addition, it will take enormous amounts of health workers' time to care for Annie. They could be spending this time on someone who was more "promising." Annie's family has asked legal authorities that they be released from any legal responsibility for her, or if that is not possible, that her life be mercifully ended.

■ What would you do if you were the legal authority? Why?
■ What should you do if you were the legal authority? Why?

To Die or Not to Die 2

Alex is a successful forty-seven-year-old businessman. He went to the doctor for a routine checkup, and the doctor found a large lump in the middle of Alex's back. Tests showed that Alex has an inoperable, malignant tumor. Radiation therapy was unsuccessful, and now Alex is in the hospital in a coma. Doctors believe that he won't live longer than six months. He will have to remain in the intensive care ward until his death. The family is able to bear the high medical expenses, but they cannot bear to see Alex this way. They ask the doctors to give Alex a lethal dose of morphine or to discontinue all medication and care and let him die naturally.

■ What would you do if you were the doctor? Why?
■ What should you do if you were the doctor? Why?

To Die or Not to Die 3

A baby is born to John and Marie. They have waited so long for a child, and both eagerly await the time when they can go home with their new arrival. The shape of the baby's head bothered a couple of the doctors, and routine tests were run to check the baby's brain waves. It was found that during the delivery, the infant suffered severe, irreversible brain damage. The baby remains in intensive care while John and Marie go home to think things over.

■ What would you do in John and Marie's situation? Why?
■ What should you do in John and Marie's situation? Why?

In the Eye of the Beholder

Susan does not think that she is attractive. People seem to avoid her, and she feels that most of the people she knows make fun of her behind her back. She comes to you for help.

- What would you do? Why?
- What should you do? Why?

If You Do, I Will

You and your brother share a bedroom. You have made it clear to your brother that he is to leave your belongings alone. You have a large tape collection and a sound system that you purchased with your own money. You come home from school one day and find many of your best tapes out gathering dust, and your favorite tape is sitting on the windowsill getting melted by the sun. You blow up at your brother. He apologizes and offers to buy a new tape, but you are still furious. You threaten to tell your parents about it and refuse to accept his apology. You tell him to get out of your room. Finally, he has had enough and says to you, "I know that you have been seeing Linda even though Mom and Dad told you not to. You have been telling them that you get off work at ten, but you really get off at nine. If you keep yelling at me and threatening me, I'm going to tell them what I know."

- What would you do? Why?
- What should you do? Why?

Yes You May; No You Won't

One evening a couple of your friends come by, and you decide to attend a movie the next weekend. You ask your parents, and although they have never heard of the movie, they give their permission. The next Friday night your friends come to the house to pick you up, and your folks ask where you are going. You remind them that they had given you permission to go to a movie. Your dad responds, "Well, I did some checking, and I was going to talk to you. I forgot you were going tonight. From what my friends tell me, the movie contains a lot of profanity and explicit sex, so I don't think you can see it. Sorry, but you can't go."

Your friends look at each other with shock and amazement. They cannot believe it. Just as they leave, you see them smile at each other like they think your folks are real losers. You are embarrassed, humiliated, and angry.

- What would you do? Why?
- What should you do? Why?

The Disappearing Failure Notice

Midterm progress reports have been mailed. The notice that Julie failed geometry will definitely not be a big hit. Since the divorce, Julie's mother has been bugging her to improve her grades. Julie tries, but she thinks Mr. Bradshaw doesn't teach geometry very well.

Julie vows to improve her grades. She knows she can do better. She asks herself, "Why upset Mom when the quarter grades don't count anyway?"

- What would you do in Julie's situation? Why?
- What should you do in Julie's situation? Why?

Caught in the Middle

Juanita corners Patti in the hall. "Patti, have you heard about Barb and Chad? They have been having sex. Can you believe it?" Patti hesitates. All four go to the same church, and Barb is a pretty good friend of hers. Patti thinks, "I have been wondering about them. It's probably true. Chad and I had sex when we went steady."

Should Patti tell Juanita she doesn't like her big mouth? Should she tell Barb the word is out? Should she confront Chad or keep quiet?

- What would you do in Patti's situation? Why?
- What should you do in Patti's situation? Why?

The Stepfather Dilemma

Denise has decided to run away. Her home life is horrible, and it is getting worse. She is afraid of her stepfather. More than once he has made sexual advances toward her. Denise is afraid to tell anyone about her fears. She doubts that her mother will believe her. She thinks that if her mother believed her, it could lead to another divorce, and one divorce is enough. Denise doesn't want anyone to know. She wonders if maybe it is her fault that her stepfather acts the way he does. Denise asks her boyfriend, Kevin, to lend her some money so she can go to live with her father in another state.

- What would you do in Denise's situation? Why?
- What would you do in Kevin's situation? Why?
- What should you do in Denise's situation? Why?
- What should you do in Kevin's situation? Why?

Why Me?

Melinda is crying because her poem was selected by the English teacher to be printed in the school yearbook. Why do things like this always happen to me? she thinks. She copied a poem out of her father's book of poetry. Never in a million years did she think something like this would happen. She is sure her father will recognize the poem.

- What would you do in Melinda's situation? Why?
- What should you do in Melinda's situation? Why?

Stretching the Truth

Kim's parents believe her again when she tells them she didn't know she was an hour late. They trust her. Kim doesn't think it is her fault that she has to stretch the truth so often. She believes she wouldn't have to lie if her parents weren't so strict. She thinks her curfew is just too early. All her friends are allowed to stay out much later. Kim has tried talking to her parents several times, but they just wouldn't listen.

- What would you do in Kim's situation? Why?
- What should you do in Kim's situation? Why?

What He Doesn't Know Won't Hurt Him

"Mom, if Jeff calls, please tell him I'm out with Tracy." Michelle wants her mother to cover for her while she goes out with Brad. Michelle doesn't want to lose Jeff, but she hates to think what will happen if he finds out she is going out with someone else. She rushes out of the house before her mother has a chance to respond.

- What would you do in Michelle's mother's situation? Why?
- What should you do in Michelle's mother's situation? Why?

No Big Deal

Kurt ditches his first-period government class to go out to breakfast with his girlfriend. A substitute teacher is showing a film he saw in another class last year. The student aid promised to mark him present. Kurt has ditched lots of classes all through high school, and he still has a 3.8 grade point average.

The substitute teacher sees Kurt and his girlfriend leaving the campus and decides to give Kurt's mother a call. That evening his mother asks him how his government class was that day.

- What would you do in Kurt's situation? Why?
- What should you do in Kurt's situation? Why?

Bart and the Bottle

Bart's locker is next to DeWayne's. One day DeWayne accidentally sees a bottle of whiskey tucked under a sweater in Bart's locker. DeWayne says hello to Bart, even though they are not good friends anymore. Bart doesn't reply. DeWayne knows all about Bart's drinking. Everyone knows Bart needs help.

DeWayne isn't sure what happened to their friendship. They used to work on the church youth council together. Until a year ago, Bart had attended church with his parents. Now they seem to have given up on him. DeWayne thinks about telling the school counselor, but ratting on Bart doesn't seem like such a great idea.

- What would you do in DeWayne's situation? Why?
- What should you do in DeWayne's situation? Why?

Did They or Didn't They?

Sharon broke up with Ron last weekend because he was pushing her to have sex. However, the word around school is that Sharon is pregnant. Sharon didn't have sex with Ron and is devastated by all the rumors. Apparently, Ron has been telling all his friends that he and Sharon were sexually active. Sharon doesn't know what to do.

- What would you do in Sharon's situation? Why?
- What should you do in Sharon's situation? Why?

See No Evil, Speak No Evil

Mark saw both boys cut the locks and steal the bikes, and the boys saw Mark. They look like gorillas as they corner him by his locker the next day. "Great," Mark thinks, "now I'm going to have my face ripped off. These guys are going to kill me." The two boys threaten Mark to keep his mouth shut or face the consequences. Mark vows never to tell anyone what he saw.

- What would you do in Mark's situation? Why?
- What should you do in Mark's situation? Why?

Truth in Lending

Brian reads, *I declare, to the best of my knowledge, that the information contained herein is true.*

The statement jumps off the page. Brian has filled out his financial aid form for college, and now he needs to sign it. In his opinion, he has not really lied—he has only underreported the amount of money he actually has in the bank. Brian's parents both have good jobs, but they do not make enough money to pay for Brian's college expenses. He will need all the financial help he can get.

- What would you do in Brian's situation? Why?
- What should you do in Brian's situation? Why?

Who Will Listen?

Casey is telling Jennifer another crude joke. Every time the girls get together, Casey has another gross joke to tell. Jennifer doesn't really like the jokes, but sometimes it is hard not to laugh—especially when everyone else does. Occasionally the jokes *are* funny. Jennifer doesn't know what to do. She wonders if she can just tell Casey to quit telling stories and walk away.

- What would you do in Jennifer's situation? Why?
- What should you do in Jennifer's situation? Why?

Read It or Watch It

Patsy has a book report due next week. She has known about it for a month now, but as usual, she has waited until the last minute. The book has been made into a movie, so Patsy decides it would be much easier to rent the video, watch it, and then do the book report from the movie. She still has time to read the book, but she knows that seeing the film would sure make it easier.

- What would you do in Patsy's situation? Why?
- What should you do in Patsy's situation? Why?

Saving Money

Thirteen years of age and younger—$1.00 off. That is what the sign at the movies says. Clint is fourteen, but he could easily pass for thirteen. His friend Joe is fourteen, too, and he cannot understand why Clint is so paranoid about telling a little white lie. Joe says that no one will get hurt, that they cannot possibly get caught, and that they could use the extra dollar to buy food once they are inside.

- What would you do in Clint's situation? Why?
- What should you do in Clint's situation? Why?

One-track Mind

"Hi, Linda, your sweater sure is looking good . . . uh . . . I mean, you're sure looking good." Todd and his three buddies look at each other and start laughing hysterically. Linda is angry. Every day during second period she has to put up with Todd's comments. His remarks always have a double meaning. Todd is a nice guy, but he seems to have only one thing on his mind.

- What would you do in Linda's situation? Why?
- What should you do in Linda's situation? Why?

Saving Face or Losing It

Kirk is making fun of Stan again. Kirk has been doing this to Stan since the sixth grade. This time it is over Stan's role in the school play. Kirk has been taunting Stan, implying that Stan is gay because he likes drama. Stan demands that Kirk meet him behind the gym after school. Stan has never been in a fight before, but he is sick of Kirk making fun of him. He has taken all he can stand, and he finally decides it's time Kirk got his. Stan can hardly wait for the end of the school day.

- What would you do in Stan's situation? Why?
- What should you do in Stan's situation? Why?

Two Dates in One

Greg asks Jenine to be his date for the upcoming junior-senior prom. She reluctantly accepts, believing it is the only offer she will get. Three days later, Max asks her to the prom. Jenine has been wanting to go out with Max for years. She cannot believe he has finally asked her. She quickly accepts, forgetting her promise to Greg. Jenine is jolted back to reality when she answers the phone and hears Greg asking what color dress she is wearing to the prom.

- What would you do in Jenine's situation? Why?
- What should you do in Jenine's situation? Why?

The Sex Talk

Heather's mom has decided to give her "the talk." She feels that sixteen-year-old Heather is ready to hear the facts of life.

When Heather's mom finishes the lecture, she gives Heather a book on sex to read and asks if she has any questions. Heather has none. She already knew everything her mother told her. She doesn't know whether she should pretend she was ignorant of the facts and ask a few questions or respond in some other way and try to communicate her feelings about sex.

- What would you do in Heather's situation? Why?
- What should you do in Heather's situation? Why?

To Tell or Not to Tell

Ever since the third grade, Lori has been Kristin's best friend. Now Lori is going steady with Kristin's older brother, Jack. Even though Jack is going steady with Lori, he is also dating another girl who attends a school across town. Kristin is the only one who knows that her brother is going out behind Lori's back. Jack asks her not to tell Lori.

- What would you do in Kristin's situation? Why?
- What should you do in Kristin's situation? Why?

Getting Even

Tammie is running for a class office at school. Someone, probably her competition, is tearing down her campaign posters almost as fast as Tammie puts them up.

Cindy, Tammie's campaign manager, thinks she saw the competition ripping down one of Tammie's posters by the cafeteria. Cindy thinks tonight would be a good time to get even. She and Tammie could tear down the competition's posters.

- What would you do in Tammie's situation? Why?
- What should you do in Tammie's situation? Why?

A Hungry Situation

Eleven brothers and sisters, an alcoholic mother, and no father—that summarizes Roger's life. He hasn't had much of a childhood. Now two of his sisters are in foster homes, and his older brother is in jail. His oldest sister got married and left home a couple of months ago. One of his sisters has a severe learning disability. Because he is the oldest boy at home, Roger feels most responsible for the family. Last semester he quit school and got a full-time job. Two weeks ago he was laid off. No jobs are available anywhere. He goes to a church for help, but they cannot do much. The family cannot get any more welfare money, and they are out of food.

Roger is considering robbing a store or breaking into a wealthy person's house to get money for his family. He has to do something soon, and robbing seems like the only option available.

- What would you do in Roger's situation? Why?
- What should you do in Roger's situation? Why?

It Is a Long Walk Home

Phil says that he isn't drunk and that he can drive Troy home with no problem. Troy knows better. He saw how much Phil had to drink.

It is late at night, and Troy knows that if he calls his parents for a ride, it may be the end of his friendship with Phil. Besides, Troy knows that his parents will tell Phil's parents. Troy considers driving Phil's car even though he doesn't have a license.

- What would you do in Troy's situation? Why?
- What should you do in Troy's situation? Why?

Working Hard or Hardly Working

Paul has to cup his hand to hide his paper from Danny. Mr. Young gives a vocabulary quiz each Friday, and every Friday Danny cheats from Paul's paper. Paul doesn't think it is fair to have to work so hard when Danny receives the same grades by cheating. So this week Paul hides his paper. Unfortunately, Mr. Young notices Paul behaving strangely and thinks that he is cheating. He embarrasses Paul in front of the class by asking what is hidden in his cupped hand.

- What should Paul do?
- What if Danny is Paul's best friend?
- What if Paul has cheated a couple of times himself by looking at someone else's paper?
- What if Danny is the first-string quarterback and needs to do well in this class to continue playing football?

There Goes the Neighborhood

The petition is plain and simple. Those signing it believe the low-income housing project should not be located in this neighborhood. Karla's father is not prejudiced, but he does worry that the "wrong" kind of people might move in and that property values will go down. He also worries that the neighborhood might become dangerous for his daughter as well as for the rest of the family. He is leaning toward signing the petition. He asks Karla for her opinion.

- What would you say in Karla's situation?
- What if a group home for the mentally retarded is the subject of the petition?
- What if a retirement home for the elderly is the subject of the petition?
- What if a home for troubled teenagers is the subject of the petition?
- What if a halfway house for paroled prisoners is the subject of the petition?

Are You Prejudiced?

Kathy's father is an elementary-school principal. He has a problem and asks Kathy for her opinion. The school needs to hire a teacher. Two equally qualified people, with the proper educational credentials, have applied for the job. One applicant is a Christian; the other is not. Kathy's father is leaning in the direction of hiring the Christian, and he wonders what Kathy thinks about that.

- What would you say in Kathy's position?
- What if one applicant is an African-American?
- What if one applicant is a woman?
- What if both applicants are women, but one is young and attractive, and the other is older and less attractive?
- What if one applicant is a disabled person?
- What if one applicant is an atheist, and the other a member of the Hare Krishnas?
- What if both applicants are *not* equally qualified—the best qualified is an atheist, and the second best is a Christian?

He Works Hard for His Money

Craig works every Saturday doing odd jobs for people. Recently, after hearing a talk in church on giving, Craig decides to give one day's wages each month to the church. He determines to start this Saturday.

After Mrs. Burt pays him, Craig stops by the store to pick up some things for his mother. He sees a tape on sale that he has wanted for a long time. He considers using the money Mrs. Burt gave him.

- What would you do in Craig's situation?
- What if Craig decides to switch weeks, buying the tape this week and giving next week's money to the church instead?
- What if a friend asks Craig to loan him some money?
- What if Craig's family needs the money?

Kicking and Screaming

Kay Lou and her friends are eating lunch at the mall. A mother and her three-year-old daughter are seated at a table near them. The little girl spills her milk on purpose, giggling as she watches her mother clean up the mess with several napkins. The girls watch as the mother slaps her daughter several times. The little girl begins to kick and scream. The mother grabs her, pulls her from her seat, and drags her out of the restaurant. The young child is kicking and screaming all the way out the door.

- What would you do in Kay Lou's situation?
- What would you do if the girl is eleven years old?
- What if the little girl spills the milk by accident?
- What if Kay Lou knows the little girl and the woman from church?
- What if the next day Kay Lou sees the little girl coming out of a house down the street and she has two black eyes?

Eye for an Eye

Molly is angry. In elementary school, kids always made fun of her because she was overweight. They never made remarks to her face, but numerous times Molly overheard her so-called best friends making fun of her. It hasn't stopped in junior high school either. They still say plenty behind her back.

The summer before she starts high school, Molly stays with her aunt in Canada. She loses thirty pounds, and the change in her is unbelievable. When she starts school in the fall, everyone is surprised. The plump Molly has suddenly become a slim, attractive long-haired redhead that all the boys want to be around. Now her friends want her friendship, but she basically tells them to get lost. She becomes a loner. Molly still has plenty of dates, but she considers all her friends phony.

- What would you do in Molly's situation?
- What if Molly's friends apologize?
- What if Molly's friends begin to call her stuck-up and aloof and try to keep boys from dating her?
- What if Molly's youth minister tells her that no matter what her best friends did to her, she has to forgive them and be friendly to them?

The Flat Tire

"I can't believe it. I knew I shouldn't have done it. Why did I do this?" Steve complains to himself.

Steve's parents loaned him their new Thunderbird to drive to the lake with his friends. He lets his girlfriend drive, even though she just received her driver's permit three weeks ago. She takes a turn a little too fast and hits the side of a mountain. A front tire blows out on impact. Luckily, no one is hurt, but the front of the car is demolished.

Steve knows that it is bad enough that his folks' new car is wrecked, but he doesn't want to think about the consequences if they find out that his girlfriend was driving. He finally decides to tell his parents that he was driving, that the tire went flat, and that he lost control of the car. It is risky, but the alternatives are a lot worse.

- What would you do in Steve's situation?
- What if Steve's girlfriend is seriously injured?
- What if it is Steve's car?
- What if, after hearing Steve's story, Steve's parents decide to sue the tire manufacturer because the tire was defective?

It Runs in the Family

Dan and Stacy are seniors at North High School. They attend the same church and are leaders both at school and at church. Dan's family supports him in his school and church activities. They attend all his functions: school plays, athletic events, and church-related activities. They are proud of their son and his accomplishments.

Stacy's family is quite a contrast. Both of her parents are alcoholics. They refuse to go to church. Stacy's father recently lost his job. Her parents never attend any of Stacy's functions. She has the leading role in the school play, but her parents don't come. When Stacy is crowned homecoming queen, her parents never show up, even though they had promised they would. In spite of her family situation, Stacy excels in all that she does.

Dan has been dating Stacy for ten months. They plan to attend a local state college because the cost is easier for Stacy to handle, and this would allow them to continue their relationship. Dan is blown away when his parents inform him that they want him to attend a private college in another state. They say they would pay all his expenses *if* he breaks up with Stacy. They point out that alcoholism might be hereditary and that Stacy comes from a background that is questionable. Dan is furious! He cannot believe his parents feel that way about Stacy, and he cannot believe that they would try to bribe him with the college offer.

■ What would you do in Dan's situation?
■ What if Dan's father has two brothers who are alcoholics?
■ What if before Dan can make a decision, Stacy finds out about his parents' wishes and breaks up with him?
■ What if Dan has always wanted to go to a private college, but had decided it was financially impossible?

A Tough Decision

Helen is twenty-eight years old and the mother of four children. She has just learned that she is pregnant again. Her husband doesn't want another child, and he insists that Helen get an abortion. Helen knows that they cannot afford another child, but the thought of getting an abortion goes against everything she believes. She is torn between her loyalty to her husband, her responsibility for the rest of her family, and her personal belief that abortion is wrong.

■ What would you do in Helen's situation?
■ What if Helen only has one other child?
■ What if an amniocentesis shows that the baby would be mentally retarded?
■ What if Helen discovers that her husband is having an affair?
■ What if Helen has fears that the pregnancy is the result of an affair she is having with another man?

Sweet Sixteen

Amber tells Mr. Hartford that she is sixteen years old. It isn't quite true, but it is close enough. She will be sixteen in seven months. Amber lied because she needs the job if she is to get a car. She wishes her parents could help her buy a car, the way all her friends' parents did. Mr. Hartford's company is the only one in town that is hiring teenagers, and she meets all the qualifications for the job except for her age.

■ What would you do in Amber's situation?
■ What if Amber will be sixteen in just one month?
■ What if Amber's father has just lost his job, and the family needs Amber's money to help them survive?

The Conflict

Sandy makes a commitment to be a part of her church's youth group. Sometimes the group's functions interfere with her social life—like tonight. There is a group planning meeting, but Sandy wants to go to the high school basketball game. Her boyfriend is playing, and he gets upset when Sandy doesn't watch him play.

- What would you do in Sandy's situation?
- What if Sandy is an elected officer of the group?
- What if the conflict is not a basketball game but homework?
- What if the conflict is a job?
- What if the conflict is a date?
- What if Sandy's brother is playing in the game?

No One Will Ever Know

Karla walks out of the store counting her change. She discovers that the cashier gave her an extra five-dollar bill by mistake. Karla cannot decide whether to return the five dollars or to keep it.

- What would you do in Karla's situation?
- What if the store has shortchanged her in the past?
- What if the store is known for its high prices and practice of ripping off customers?
- What if she has been given a twenty-dollar bill instead?
- What if just as Karla is getting in the car to leave, she sees the grocery checker standing outside, frantically looking around as though he has discovered his mistake?

Forgetful

Sonya worked for Juan last weekend because he needed the time off to attend camp. He promised to work Sonya's hours the next weekend in exchange for the favor. When Juan made the promise to Sonya, he had forgotten that he is supposed to sing in a musical that next Sunday. Sonya has already scheduled a trip to the lake.

- What would you do in Juan's situation?
- What if Juan had forgotten he has a date with his girlfriend and her parents that weekend?
- What if Juan had forgotten that his father wants him to work around the house that weekend?
- What if Juan is coming down with the chicken pox and is contagious?

Special-Order Baby

The Johnsons are a typical middle-class, white couple in their late twenties. They really want a child but are unable to have one. They tried to adopt, but they were told that they would be put on a waiting list and that it might be several years until they would be given a child. Their attorney arranges for a surrogate mother to be artificially inseminated with Mr. Johnson's sperm. She will carry the baby to full term, and once it is delivered, she will give the baby to the Johnsons. The contract is signed.

Nine months later, the baby is born to the surrogate mother, and the baby is severely mentally retarded.

- What would you do in the Johnsons' situation?
- What would you do in the surrogate mother's situation?
- As the Johnsons, what would you do if the baby is perfectly normal and the surrogate mother decides to keep it?

A Friendly Lunch

The four girls are supposed to have lunch together at the mall before going shopping. Samantha has invited Carol. Laura and Mindy demand that she tell Carol she is not invited. Laura and Mindy don't like Carol. They say that Carol used to be okay until she started getting into religion. Now Laura and Mindy feel uncomfortable with Carol. Even though Carol is Samantha's friend, Samantha also feels uncomfortable with her, so she doesn't mind cancelling the lunch date. Her friendship with Laura and Mindy is more important to her than her friendship with Carol.

So Samantha calls, "Carol, this is Samantha. We decided to cancel our lunch at the mall. Mindy's parents said she couldn't go. I'll see you Sunday at church. Bye." Samantha is glad that that is over.

The lunch is fun. Samantha, Laura, and Mindy really have a good time. No one even misses Carol until Samantha spots her walking toward their table. Mindy and Laura quickly excuse themselves and leave. Samantha sits staring as Carol walks up.

- What would you do in Carol's situation? What would you say to Samantha? What would you say to Laura and Mindy?
- What would you do in Samantha's situation? What would you say to Carol? What would you say to Laura and Mindy?

The Playmate Locker

Everyone seems to like Paul. He isn't a crude person, but his locker is full of pornographic magazines. He took them from his father's study without his dad knowing. He tapes one of the centerfolds inside his locker, and it becomes the main attraction during lunch.

Angelo's locker is next to Paul's. They are sort of locker friends. Angelo has never really seen much porno stuff, but as he thinks about it, it sounds intriguing. Angelo's folks would flip out if they knew he had ever seen a porno magazine, but Angelo sees nothing wrong with looking as long as it doesn't lead to anything.

Paul comes up to Angelo's locker. "Hey, Angelo, what's happening? I've invited a bunch of my friends over this weekend for a video night. We're going to show some X-rated stuff. Interested?" Angelo doesn't know what to say.

- What would you do in Angelo's situation? What would you say to Paul?

- What would you do if you were Angelo's girlfriend and he tells you he is going to the video night?
- What would you do if you were Paul's girlfriend and found out about his interest in pornography?
- What would you do if you were Paul's parents and found out about his interest in pornography?

Do Me a Favor

Jill needs a promotion. Her first year of college requires a lot more money than she is making, and tuition is going up next semester. When Rick, Jill's boss, first mentions the possibility of a promotion and a pay raise, Jill is excited. But the more Rick talks, the more Jill realizes there are strings attached.

"Jill, I really think I need to know you better before I can decide whether you should get the promotion. My wife is going out of town this weekend. I wondered if you would like to come over to the house for a few drinks and dinner. I would understand, of course, if you couldn't make it, but I do need to decide on the promotion this week-end." Jill has never had anything like this happen before. She doesn't know what to do.

Barbara, Jill's best friend, encourages Jill to accept the dinner offer. She advises her to lead Rick on without yielding sexually and then to drop him when she gets the promotion.

Sandy, Jill's older sister, disagrees. She recommends that Jill go to Rick's supervisor and complain of sexual harassment. Jill had thought of that but is afraid Rick would deny everything, and then she would not only lose the promotion but her present job as well. She really doesn't know what to do.

- What would you do in Jill's situation?
- What would you do to help Jill?
- Imagine you are Jill's boyfriend; what would you do?
- Imagine you are one of Jill's parents; what would you do?
- Do you agree that Jill is being sexually harassed? If not, how would you define sexual harassment?

Whose Life Do You Support?

Tyrone's thoughts of Grandma Thornton are good ones. He really loves her. Tyrone feels lucky to have a grandmother like her.

Tyrone has been accepted at a good Catholic college. Since it is a private school and tuition is high, his grandmother said she would pay for it. But she had a stroke recently and is in a coma. The doctor says she will die, although it could be months before she does. The life-support system that is keeping her alive is expensive, and if Tyrone's grandmother remains in a coma for months, all her money will be spent on the hospital bills.

Tyrone's father is considering asking the doctor to remove the life-support equipment and allow Grandma Thornton to die.

- If you were Tyrone's father, what would you do?
- If you were Tyrone, what would you suggest your father do?
- If you were the doctor, what would you suggest?

On the Outside Looking In

The youth group is not at all like the group Maggie belonged to back home. Maggie and her mother moved after the divorce because Maggie's mother wanted to be closer to her family for support. So here she is. It is her fourth Sunday visiting Saint Andrew's. "Visiting," because Maggie doesn't yet feel like part of the group. Her mom knows several people in the church, but Maggie is getting the feeling that she will never get to know anyone. It seems that the kids in the group are nothing like the kids in her old youth group. In fact, they are just as cold as the kids at her new high school.

A guy named Scott seems totally interested in his girlfriend, and the two of them are inseparable. They hold hands during singing, group discussions, games, everything! Then there is Sarah. She is either combing her hair or checking her makeup, and the games she plays with the guys are unbelievable! Tom sits in the corner. People at school call him "chemical head." The church kids ignore him, but he doesn't seem to care. Then there is Fred, who has to tell everyone all about his weekend exploits. He parties hard and is proud of his fast life. Today he has an audience of ninth graders listening to his Friday night story. Karen always keeps her nose in the Bible. She is so involved with her Bible that she forgets about people. Today Maggie ends up sitting next to the three gossipers. Their conversation is like a soap opera.

As far as Maggie can tell, most of the people in the group act as if they are there because their parents made them attend.

- What would you do in Maggie's situation? What would you say to the rest of the group? To your mother?
- Does Maggie see any difference between the people at school and the people in the youth group? What might this tell you about Maggie?
- How could this youth group make Maggie feel a part of it?
- Is there anything wrong with having a certain group of friends that you enjoy being around more than others?

Heartthrob

Dear Diary,

Today was so great! Chai Ling wants to go steady. He is a totally hot guy. *And* he's a senior! I can't believe it. Any girl in school would give her virginity away for him—and he likes me. I am soooooooooo happy. Heather is totally jealous and being a real dork. I don't care.

Of course, it's going to take some real doing to pull this off. You know why! My parents are the nerds of the universe! They don't want me dating seniors. My parents actually think every senior guy wants to rape every ninth-grade girl. Well, they're wrong. Chai is the neatest guy I have ever met, and I am not going to let him go. I mean, I wouldn't even mind having sex with him, he turns me on so much. What's wrong with having sex with someone you really like? Nothing. And besides, if I'm going to keep him around for four years, we can't exactly hold hands. Seriously, Diary, I would marry him right now. Of course I can't, I'm only fifteen—but my mom was eighteen when she married my dad. Whoops, gotta go, Chai's calling.

Darla

- What would you do in Darla's situation? Why?
- What should you do in Darla's situation? Why?
- What should Darla's parents do?

Teenage Mom

Dear Diary,

I don't believe my mother. It's like she thinks she is sixteen or something. I need a million clothes, and I come home today and she is totally dressed like a teenager. She looks better than I do! I'm serious. When I say something like I think she looks ridiculous or I think she looks too young, she goes crazy. She gets all mad and says that everyone dresses like that—which they don't. She says that she has the right, after all these years, to buy herself some clothes and that it is okay for a mom to want to look nice. Gee, Mom, no kidding. She doesn't even listen. It's embarrassing. And she is always wanting me to invite all the girls over so *we* can do something together. Can you believe it? I don't want my mom to do things with me and my girl-friends. I've even tried to talk to Dad about it. You know what he says? "I *like* your mom to look young." Totally sick! Why don't they just try to look like a mom and a dad instead of trying to look like they are still in their teens?

Becky

- What should Becky do?
- What should Becky's mom do?
- If you were Becky, what would you tell your father?

Soaps and Sex

Dear Diary,

My mom totally blew up at me today. Yep, you got it. Soaps. She told me never to watch soaps, but she is always gone, and you know how much I like soaps. It's like I'm addicted. Well, she came home early today from work and caught me. I got the all-time lecture once again. "Don't you know they're bad for you? All they show is sex, sex, sex. Everyone in those soaps is sleeping around." She was really mad this time. I just sat there and agreed with her. I mean, what's the use? I don't really agree with her. I mean, I know they do have a lot of sex, and everyone is sleeping with everyone, but I know it isn't real life. I know it's wrong. But I'm not going to watch soaps and then become a pervert. They're just fun to watch. Besides, all the guys are total babes.

Lauren

- What would you do in Lauren's situation? Why?
- What should you do in Lauren's situation? Why?
- If you were Lauren's mom, what would you say to Lauren about soaps?

PART 2

Forming an Opinion

Introduction

In the case studies presented in this section, each character takes a definite stand on an issue or voices a clear opinion. The young people who are analyzing these case studies are asked how they feel about the character's opinion or the situation that is described and to explore their own reasons for the stand that they take. The process used here asks the participants to move from feelings to reason, from heart to head. The aim, of course, is to have the heart and the head in concert. This is a challenging task for all Christians.

The sources of young people's opinions are many: The received and unanalyzed values of their family or church; opinions in reaction to family or church opinion; agreement with their peers' opinions or those promoted by the media and advertising. Also, age and maturity will alter the views of young people. The close and careful awareness of individually chosen opinions will be more common among older high school students than among younger people, whose concern for conformity will be greater.

In this exploration of opinions and reasons, the same responsibility falls to the youth minister, that is, to offer young people the gospel values that anchor opinions or that can cause or impel a change of opinion. Although no person can force moral choice or action, the mature Christian community and mature individuals can and must provide young people with the gospel values that the church and its individual members hold, cherish, and offer.

This Can't Be Happening

I can't believe it. My parents are getting a divorce. My mom says it's because Dad is working all the time and doesn't care about her. But what about me? It seems like neither of them care about me. Why do they have to do this *now?* It really screws up my senior year. They could have waited until I was in college. Sure, I knew they weren't happy, but so what? At least *I* was happy. Now we're *all* unhappy. Besides, they can move or get another job, but what can I do? Change schools my senior year? Get a job? Give me a break. I am really angry at my parents for being so selfish that they can't even think of what this is doing to me.

Rick, 18

How do you feel about Rick's statement?

Strongly agree	Agree	Neutral	Disagree	Strongly disagree

- If you agree, what would you add to the statement above?
- If you disagree, why?

Change of Mind

When I was in junior high, I thought people who took drugs were stupid. I still do if you are talking about stoners. But now that I'm in high school, I think drugs are just like anything else—if you abuse them, they are bad; if you don't abuse them, they can be okay. I smoke a joint now and then, but not during school or when I'm driving or even every time there is a party. Just once in a while. It's not as bad as everyone says. My parents would totally flip out if they knew I had *ever* smoked before. But, hey, they drink and it ain't no big deal.

Brad, 18, senior

How do you feel about Brad's statement?

Strongly agree	Agree	Neutral	Disagree	Strongly disagree

- If you agree, what would you add to the statement above?
- If you disagree, why?

Be True to Your Friends

Look. Everyone lies. It's just part of being a teenager. If by lying you can keep your folks happy and keep your school and your life under control, then why not? I don't mean that it's okay to lie all the time. And I don't think you should lie to your friends, because once you do that and your friends find out—well, you won't have any friends. Here is the way I look at it: When you're in high school, everyone's on your case—your parents, your teachers, your boss at work—and you *have* to keep them off your back. The only protection you and I have against all that pressure is to lie once in a while.

Brenda, 17, junior

How do you feel about Brenda's statement?

Strongly agree	Agree	Neutral	Disagree	Strongly disagree

- If you agree, what would you add to the statement above?
- If you disagree, why?

Never Admit More Than They Know

Here is my philosophy. When your mom or dad, a teacher, or some other adult confronts you or starts questioning you about something they think you have done, deny it all first. Then if they confront you with some obvious fact, admit to that, but nothing else. Deny everything else. For example, if my folks came in and confronted me because I got in late the night before, the discussion would go something like this:

Parents: What time did you get in last night, Craig? You were supposed to be home at midnight.

Craig: I *was* home at midnight—or maybe ten minutes after. I didn't look at my watch.

Parents: It must have been more than ten minutes, Craig, because I woke up at 12:45 and checked, and you still weren't home.

Craig: Well, it *might* have been that late. But I know I left the party way before twelve so I would be home on time.

Parents: Was there any drinking going on at the party?

Craig: I sure didn't see any.

Parents: Mrs. Johnson said she had to send a whole bunch of guys away from the party who had stashed some booze in the front bushes and were drinking out on the front lawn.

Craig: Maybe—I don't know. I was inside the house the whole time.

It's a great strategy. It works every time. Only admit what they know and deny everything else.

Craig, 17, junior

How do you feel about Craig's statement?

Strongly agree	Agree	Neutral	Disagree	Strongly disagree

- If you agree, what would you add to the statement above?
- If you disagree, why?

Mellow Fellow

I think this Christian stuff is cool. Seriously, I think it's great—as long as you don't get too weird about it. I like our youth group. We have a great youth minister and a super-neat program at our church, and that is all great. But when they start saying we ought to go to church every week and help out with service projects—come on, who has time for that stuff? You can do that when you are older. Besides, as long as the youth group keeps you off the streets and gives you a good time, what else do you need? If someone wants to be a priest some day, great; but I don't think I should feel guilty just because I don't want to. When you are in high school, you have a lot to do—and church ought to be a part of what you do, but only a part. Life is a lot more than going to church.

Roger, 16, sophomore

How do you feel about Roger's statement?

Strongly agree	Agree	Neutral	Disagree	Strongly disagree

- If you agree, what would you add to the statement?
- If you disagree, why?

What's Important?

You know what's important? I'll tell you. Making the bucks. It always makes people mad when I say that, but they only get mad because it's true. Making a living, that's it. That's the bottom line. You need money to buy a car, have nice clothes, get an apartment or a house, and do fun things. That's what life is about. Who runs the country? Who runs the churches? Who runs everything? The people with the bucks, that's who. Anyone who tells you anything else is a liar.

Connor, 16, sophomore

How do you feel about Connor's statement?

Strongly agree	Agree	Neutral	Disagree	Strongly disagree

- If you agree, what would you add to the statement above?
- If you disagree, why?

Nuclear Pie

To listen to all these sociologist types talk, you would think all the teenagers in the world were sitting around totally afraid that the bomb is going to drop. What a joke. None of my friends sit around worrying about a nuclear holocaust. They *do* worry that they won't get their piece of the pie, but that's about it. We are not antinuclear as much as we are anti-anything-that-keeps-us-from-living-the-good-life. All we care about is that we get to grow up and have a good time; whatever keeps us from doing that, we are against.

Serena, 15, sophomore

How do you feel about Serena's statement?

| Strongly agree | Agree | Neutral | Disagree | Strongly disagree |

- If you agree, what would you add to the statement above?
- If you disagree, why?

Negative Outlook

Every time I do something wrong, my parents remind me of all the things I have done wrong in the last two years. They never forget and seldom forgive. They always focus on the negative. I can do everything I am supposed to for three weeks in a row and they never say a word. But make one mistake and I never stop hearing about it. I don't think they have ever said a positive thing to me. It doesn't matter what I do—they are never satisfied.

Arlin, 14, ninth grader

How do you feel about Arlin's statement?

| Strongly agree | Agree | Neutral | Disagree | Strongly disagree |

- If you agree, what would you add to the statement above?
- If you disagree, why?

It Is My Body

It is *my* body. I don't understand why my parents think they can tell me what to do with my body. I'm old enough now to know what is good for me and what isn't. Besides, I usually don't get in arguments with my folks about what is *good* for me; it's usually just a matter of taste. And my taste is just as right as theirs. When it comes to my hairstyle, my earring, or any other part of my personal appearance, I think that should be *my* choice, not my parents'.

Seth, 15, sophomore

How do you feel about Seth's statement?

| Strongly agree | Agree | Neutral | Disagree | Strongly disagree |

- If you agree, what would you add to the statement above?
- If you disagree, why?

I Don't Want to Die

I don't care what they say in church about heaven; I don't want to die. It may be great up there, but I like it here just fine. I don't want to go to heaven right now. I don't want to sit around with a bunch of angels. I want to live and have fun right now. If that means I'm not a Christian, then I guess I'm not a Christian. Because I don't think anyone should want to die rather than live.

Kendra, 16, sophomore

How do you feel about Kendra's statement?

| Strongly agree | Agree | Neutral | Disagree | Strongly disagree |

- If you agree, what would you add to the statement above?
- If you disagree, why?

Don't Knock Rock

I cannot believe so many adults get bent out of shape over rock music. I bet 99 percent of the kids never even listen to the words. I don't. I might even know the words to some songs by heart, but I still don't really think about them that much. Oh, yeah, sure, there are some heavy-metal freaks running around with Metallica and AC/DC T-shirts, but I don't think they listen to the words either.

Cal, 18, senior

How do you feel about Cal's statement?

| Strongly agree | Agree | Neutral | Disagree | Strongly disagree |

- If you agree, what would you add to the statement above?
- If you disagree, why?

Sex Is for Everyone

Nobody waits until they are married to have sex anymore. Nobody. Except maybe somebody who grew up on an island where there wasn't anybody of the other sex—or maybe somebody who lies a lot. Sure you have to be careful—but having sex is just a normal part of relationships nowadays.

Jean, 17, junior

How do you feel about Jean's statement?

Strongly agree	Agree	Neutral	Disagree	Strongly disagree

- If you agree, what would you add to the statement above?
- If you disagree, why?

After Sex, Then What?

I had sex with this guy. It wasn't great, but I still liked it. Anyway, I felt guilty about it, and I even broke up with the guy. Our priest said that God did forgive me but that I should never do it again. *I know* I shouldn't have sex again, but every time I go out with a new guy I want to. I can't help it. I've tried to keep from having sex, but once you've experienced it, you can't exactly go back to holding hands. Anyone who thinks you can have sex and then not have it anymore is crazy.

Tina, 16, junior

How do you feel about Tina's statement?

Strongly agree	Agree	Neutral	Disagree	Strongly disagree

- If you agree, what would you add to the statement above?
- If you disagree, why?

Picky Parents

My parents are paranoid. Every time I come home from a party, they want to know if there was any drinking or drugs. Well, of course, there was. You can't go to a party anymore without someone drinking or smoking dope, but I don't drink and I don't do drugs. My folks should believe me. If my parents knew what half of my friends did, they wouldn't let me have anything to do with them. But I can't tell my parents what really goes on; they would lock me in chains and only let me out of the house to go to school. I wish they would just trust me and realize that what my *friends* do doesn't affect what *I* do.

Dana, 15, sophomore

How do you feel about Dana's statement?

Strongly agree	Agree	Neutral	Disagree	Strongly disagree

- If you agree, what would you add to the statement above?
- If you disagree, why?

School Is No Big Deal

My parents are more concerned about how I do in school than anything else in my life. They are always pressuring me to take college prep courses and get straight *A*'s. Well, I don't feel that way. School is okay, and I'm smart enough to get decent grades, but I'm tired of the pressure. I don't think you learn all that much in high school anyway. Besides, most of the teachers couldn't care less about education. They just collect their paychecks. I just don't think you need to panic about grades. I'll get serious about school later. Right now I want to enjoy my high school years. So my SAT's aren't great, so what? I can always go to a junior college or not go to college at all for a while. In fact, a bunch of my friends and I are talking about traveling around Europe for a year after we graduate from high school. Our parents are totally freaking out at that idea.

Linda, 18, senior

How do you feel about Linda's statement?

| Strongly agree | Agree | Neutral | Disagree | Strongly disagree |

- If you agree, what would you add to the statement above?
- If you disagree, why?

Phony Kids

High school kids are so phony. You go to a class or a conference on racism or hunger, and kids sit around crying and saying how concerned they are. Then when the class is over, you see the same kids making fun of some other kid and talking about all the new clothes they "need" right now. My friends only care about themselves. They *say* they are not going to be like their parents, that they are going to care about the world, and hunger, and nuclear war—but as soon as school is over, they are back to thinking about themselves full-time. None of my friends think a thing about inconveniencing their parents or asking for more money. In fact, they get mad if their parents won't go out of their way to help them. We're a bunch of spoiled, selfish, self-centered little brats. We pretend to care about the world, but really we don't care about anything except money, clothes, our friends, our music, and having a good time.

Claudia, 18, senior

How do you feel about Claudia's statement?

| Strongly agree | Agree | Neutral | Disagree | Strongly disagree |

- If you agree, what would you add to the statement above?
- If you disagree, why?

Old-fashioned

I guess I'm old-fashioned, but I really do think there is a hell. I don't think I'm better than my friends who don't belong to any church or seem to have no faith in God. I don't think they are horrible people—I just care about them. I'm one of those weirdos who loves God. I know that people who don't believe in Christ are nice people, but I truly feel they would be happier if they believed in God. Even though people make fun of me, I think I should try to tell all my friends about Jesus. And if they don't like it, that's all right—they still need to hear about him.

Bruce, 15, ninth grader

How do you feel about Bruce's statement?

Strongly agree	Agree	Neutral	Disagree	Strongly disagree

- If you agree, what would you add to the statement above?
- If you disagree, why?

The Beautiful People

I go to this humongous church. It is *the* place to go. We have about two thousand families and about two hundred high school kids in the youth group. All the kids in the group are really popular at school. Our youth minister is good-looking, athletic, and a good speaker. We have the greatest programs and the greatest camps. We have lots of money in our youth budget, and the adults in the church really support us. We have a lot of really neat social-action mission projects, too.

There is just one problem. The whole thing is a fraud. Maybe *joke* is a better word. I'm not saying the kids are phonies—I'm just saying that church is just another social club. The kids in the youth group hang around together at school and go to the same parties. There isn't one bit of difference between the kids in our youth group and the rest of the kids in school. They have sex with their girlfriends or boyfriends, they make fun of people, they swear, they drink, they go to R-rated movies. They do everything that everyone else does, except that they go to church. At church they say all the right things. It's not like they are being hypocrites; it's just that they don't see any problem—you go to church and behave one way, and you go to school and behave another way. I think it's a bunch of baloney. Why even go to church if it's just another place to go? I don't go anymore. At least I feel more honest.

Gerald, 16, junior

How do you feel about Gerald's statement?

Strongly agree	Agree	Neutral	Disagree	Strongly disagree

- If you agree, what would you add to the statement above?
- If you disagree, why?

Immoral Majority

I have this friend who goes to a real conservative church. His youth group decided to protest the sale of *Playboy* and *Penthouse* at the local minimart. So they had this big demonstration, and it worked—the store decided to quit selling those magazines. I think that was stupid. I'm against pornography, but what's wrong with *Playboy* and *Penthouse?* We see just as much nudity in most of the movies we go to. And, besides, I don't think we should force our beliefs on other people.

Shannon, 14, ninth grader

How do you feel about Shannon's statement?

Strongly agree	Agree	Neutral	Disagree	Strongly disagree

- If you agree, what would you add to the statement above?
- If you disagree, why?

Just Waiting

Yes, I like the fact that my folks have money. I like having a car, a nice house, and nice clothes. I enjoy all those things. But if my parents think I'm going to be like them, they are wrong. I've made up my mind that when I get older, I'm not going to do the Big American Dream thing. I'm not going to get a job so I can buy a house in suburbia, get my Volvo station wagon, and have 2.3 kids. As soon as I get out of college, I'm going to some third world country, live in a tent, and give my life to helping people. I enjoy the good things in life, but I also hate what they do to me and my parents. I'm not going to let that happen. My folks would die if they knew how I really feel, so I don't tell them. I'm just waiting until I'm old enough to do what I want.

Ken, 16, sophomore

How do you feel about Ken's statement?

Strongly agree	Agree	Neutral	Disagree	Strongly disagree

- If you agree, what would you add to the statement above?
- If you disagree, why?

No Difference

Debbie dates guys of all religions and of no religion. Her mother doesn't like this. Debbie explains to her mom that the guys she dates are no different from those who are Catholic. (What she really wants to tell her mother is that sometimes the Catholic guys are *worse!*) Her mother finds this disturbing. She argues that other parents also agree that it would be better if Debbie dates only Catholic guys.

- How do you feel about this situation?
- What is the main issue in this situation?
- What should be done about this situation?

Confidentiality

Dr. Morton prescribed birth control pills to sixteen-year-old Dawn at her request. Dr. Morton wonders if she should call Dawn's parents and inform them. Dr. Morton feels guilty. She has been the family's doctor for years.

- How do you feel about this situation?
- What is the main issue in this situation?
- What should be done about this situation?

Driving While Intoxicated

Jack feels numb. His father told him this morning that his best friend, Charlie, was instantly killed last night when a drunk driver hit him head-on. The driver was arrested. It is the third time he has been caught driving while intoxicated.

- How do you feel about this situation?
- What is the main issue in this situation?
- What should be done about this situation?

Under Control

Occasionally, Randy smokes pot and drinks a few beers at parties with his friends. He always stays in control, and he never drives if he feels intoxicated. Randy believes that he is acting responsibly and that he can quit pot and alcohol any time he wants to. Many kids use drugs or drink before and after school. Randy only does it on weekends. He doesn't see it as a problem. It never interferes with his schoolwork, home life, job, or church.

- How do you feel about this situation?
- What is the main issue in this situation?
- What should be done about this situation?

Hunger Hurts

A baby died in her arms.

Seventeen-year-old Lisa had taken a trip to Haiti with her Aunt Glenda. Every year, Aunt Glenda went to Haiti to donate two weeks of her time to help the poor people.

Lisa had heard about hunger and starvation, but never in her wildest imagination had she dreamed poverty could be so terrible. Lisa had never been hungry in her life, nor had she known anyone who was starving. She felt sick to her stomach as well as guilty, selfish, and angry. She felt guilty because she had so much and had never helped anyone in need before. It wasn't easy to admit that she might be selfish. She was angry and felt that it wasn't fair for these people to have so little when she had so much.

Now Lisa stands there with the lifeless baby in her arms, gone because he didn't have enough to eat. Tears fill her eyes. She wants to scream or run or go home and tell everyone to quit being so selfish. Lisa's confusion and helplessness overwhelm her. Hugging the baby, she just sits down in the dirt and cries.

■ How do you feel about this situation?
■ What is the main issue in this situation?
■ What should be done about this situation?

Home, Sweet Home

Jim is working at the rest home for a summer job. The conditions in there are horrid, and the smell is unbearable. Jim wonders how people could work there, let alone live there. He is shocked by the way the older people are treated, but he does not know what to do. The rest home has passed all the health inspections that are necessary for it to remain in operation, but something *has* to be wrong. Either someone was paid off, or some health inspector was terribly negligent. He wonders if the owners simply fixed up the home whenever they knew an inspection team was coming. Whatever the reason, Jim decides that something has to be done. However, he does not know what that something should be.

■ How do you feel about this situation?
■ What is the main issue in this situation?
■ What should be done about this situation?

What Is Justice?

There is no justice anymore. At least, Paulo doesn't believe there is. His home was recently robbed, and a police officer was shot while trying to arrest the thief. There was a scuffle. When the police officer tried to reach for his gun, the thief's gun accidentally went off and the police officer was hit. The judge dismissed the case because of insufficient evidence. The police officer lived, but he will be disabled for life.

- How do you feel about this situation?
- What is the main issue in this situation?
- What should be done about the result?

Boycott

David received a letter in the mail from a national organization asking him to boycott a company's products. The letter explains that this multinational corporation advertises some of its products during TV shows that have too much sex and violence. David considers participating in the boycott. He believes that something needs to be done about the sex and violence on television.

- How do you feel about this situation?
- What is the main issue in this situation?
- What should be done about this situation?

Sex, Drugs, and Rock 'n' Roll

"Sex, drugs, and rock 'n' roll. That's all today's youth think is important," Mr. Marshall complains. He is seated in the teacher's lounge talking with the other teachers during break. "Most kids never study, and even if they do, they only study enough to get a grade so they can get their parents off their backs—*if* they still live with their real parents. Most kids don't know how to read or spell, and they don't care. All they care about is the weekend, getting stoned, and walking around like zombies with their cassette stereos blasting their eardrums out." Mr. Marshall is wound up now.

One of the teachers looks at Mr. Marshall disgustedly and says, "Then why don't you quit teaching, Marshall?"

- How do you feel about this situation?
- What is the main issue in this situation?
- What should be done about this situation?

There Has to Be a Better Way

Until his church's summer camp, Chip could not seem to motivate himself to pray. At camp, he made a commitment to pray every day. He kept that commitment for about three weeks. Now, six months later, he wonders if he is even a Christian. He hasn't prayed for months, and he can't seem to pray even though he really tries. He has talked with the assistant priest at Holy Rosary, who told him that all he has to do is ask God for help. Father told Chip that if he wanted to pray, eventually he would. But that didn't work either.

- How do you feel about this situation?
- What is the main issue in this situation?
- What should be done about this situation?

Who Can You Turn To?

Trudy feels so alone. She is facing a tough problem and needs advice from an adult. No one close to her will listen, and she cannot find anyone to help her with her burden. Her stomach aches. She wants to talk to her mother, but she already has enough to worry about with the divorce and the new job. Trudy finds it so hard to face her problem by herself. She wishes she could find someone who cares enough to listen.

- How do you feel about this situation?
- What is the main issue in this situation?
- What should be done about this situation?

Waiting

When Cally broke up with Will, she thought she could never love anyone again. Cally had believed she was in love. It had felt like the real thing, and she had been so happy.

Cally finally got over Will, but now she is lonely. She has not dated for quite a while. Cally wants to date but hasn't had any offers. Cally is tired of waiting, tired of staying home on weekends, and especially tired of being lonely. Cally's friend tells her that her lack of dates is God's will, and she should be patient. Cally thinks this advice sounds like a bunch of bunk.

- How do you feel about this situation?
- What is the main issue in this situation?
- What should be done about this situation?

The Rip-off

Over the past weekend, thirty-seven lockers at Benton High School were vandalized. Floyd's locker was one of them. He is furious that someone would do such a thing. He feels that nothing is safe anymore. Floyd is told that the school's insurance will cover the cost of the stolen items. The insurance agent asks the students to list their stolen goods, supply an accurate description of each item, and return the report to her. She does not question them about their itemized lists; she believes that the students can be trusted. The principal thinks that the agent should question the students thoroughly because he believes that most students will be tempted to pad their list to receive more insurance money.

The principal is right. Floyd lies about a radio being stolen. Eventually he receives money for the radio.

Wilma, whose locker is above Floyd's, reports truthfully that nothing of value was stolen from her locker. She knows that Floyd lied.

- How do you feel about this situation?
- What is the main issue in this situation?
- What should be done about this situation?

Party Time

Owen's parents see nothing wrong with drinking. In fact, they see nothing wrong with Owen drinking, as long as they are with him when he drinks. They feel that their presence in the room keeps their son from abusing alcohol. That is why Owen's mom is so upset when she unexpectedly comes home early and finds Owen picking up beer cans around the house. It is obvious that he has cut school to host an impromptu party with a group of friends. "I can't believe you would do this, Owen. You can drink anytime you want to when we are home. Wait until your father gets home. You are grounded."

While cleaning up the mess, Owen overhears his mother on the phone. She is calling the parents of his friends who were at the party. His friends are going to hate him.

- How do you feel about this situation?
- What is the main issue in this situation?
- What should be done about this situation?

A School Night's Secret Meeting

Bonnie's mother will not let her use the car for social events on school nights. If she needs to go to the library or to a meeting for church or school, the use of the car is no problem.

Tonight Jeff will be at a birthday party for Katrina. Bonnie has been waiting for the opportunity to meet him, and at last she will have the chance, except she has no way to get to Katrina's house because it is a school night. Katrina tells Bonnie that she could easily get the car by telling her mom she needs to go to the library. Bonnie agrees.

On the way to Katrina's house, Bonnie stops at the library to check out a book. She doesn't feel that she is lying now because she did go to the library.

- How do you feel about this situation?
- What is the main issue in this situation?
- What should be done about this situation?

God and Rock 'n' Roll

Brendan and Tony were really surprised when they arrived at the youth group meeting last night and heard the guest speaker discuss rock 'n' roll. He suggested rock 'n' roll music was from the devil. He said the words and the beat were sinful and suggestive and that many songs used "backward masking" to hide sinister messages.

Tony's parents don't like him listening to rock 'n' roll, and they keep telling him that he should not listen to it.

Brendan thinks the whole thing is ridiculous. He is into hard rock and even has some records by so-called satanic groups. He believes that even though some of the words are bad, the groups do whatever they think will make money. He believes that the groups that talk about Satan just do it to get media attention. Even though some groups see nothing wrong with drugs and may even encourage drug taking, Brendan feels that he is intelligent enough to reject that kind of thinking.

- Which person or persons do you most agree with: Brendan, Tony's parents, or the youth group speaker?
- Does God care what kind of music you listen to?
- Do the words in music affect you? How?

A Disturbing Issue

There was no telling how the class stumbled upon the subject of nuclear war, but however it happened, Ellen found herself arguing with the teacher. Ellen believes it is time the United States took a stronger stand on limiting the number of nuclear bombs it builds. She feels that a nuclear freeze is needed and that the United States should stop developing bombs. The teacher disagrees. She argues that the United States can only maintain peace through strength and that this strength prevents other nations from involving the world in a nuclear war.

Jamie defends Ellen by arguing that the United States' strength does not lie in the number of bombs it possesses. He says that already too many bombs exist and that the strength of the nation lies in its faith in God and its strong morality.

Ricardo thinks the whole discussion is a joke. He feels that nothing can be done about the buildup of nuclear weapons, so there is no use trying to prevent it.

Alicia, upset that the teacher and class members are discussing the nuclear issue, leaves the room. She believes the class should be discussing spiritual things, not nuclear bombs.

- Does the nuclear issue have anything to do with Christianity and the Bible?
- Does the church have a point of view on this issue, or are you free to hold almost any viewpoint regarding the nuclear issue?
- How would you respond to Ellen?
- How would you respond to the teacher?
- How would you respond to Jamie?
- How would you respond to Ricardo?
- How would you respond to Alicia?

PART 3

Ranking Actions and Decisions

Introduction

The more complex case studies offered in this section ask the young people to make judgments about the decisions and the actions of each character. In working with young people on these exercises, emphasize that the judgment is on the *decisions* and the *actions* of individuals, not on the individuals themselves. Also keep in mind that young people need help assuming responsibility for their actions. It is easy and unhelpful for young people (and all people, for that matter) to blame others for their situation in life and for their actions. The guiding principle here is that each person is responsible for his or her own actions. However, others who are involved with the person who is experiencing difficulty can fail to truly be helpful, and here judgments about others' actions can be made and analyzed.

Be Home by Ten

Susan and Tina are having a great time at the church youth group social. After the social, the two girls are spending the night together at Tina's. While waiting to watch a film at the social, Susan remembers that her mother told her to be back from the social by 10:00 p.m. Her mother has always been strict. Susan announces to the group that she cannot stay for the film because it won't be over until 10:30 p.m. A few of her friends are annoyed. They argue that Susan's mother will never know if Susan stays out a few minutes late because Susan is spending the night at Tina's. Susan finally agrees with them. She makes Tina promise not to say a word to Susan's mother. The two girls stay for the movie, after which they arrive at Tina's house about 10:55 p.m. Susan and Tina visit for a while and then go to sleep.

The next day, as the two girls are getting ready to go shopping, the phone rings. Tina answers it and is surprised by the voice of Susan's mother, who wants to know if the girls had a fun evening. Tina tells her they had a wonderful time. As the conversation is ending, Susan's mom asks what time the girls arrived home. Tina tells her that they came home around 10:00 p.m.

Tina's mother overhears the phone conversation. She knows what time the girls really arrived home. She decides that it is none of her business and stays out of the situation rather than talk to the girls or call Susan's mother with the truth.

- Rank the choices of the following characters from best to worst: Tina, Susan, Susan's mother, friends in the group, Tina's mother.
- Provide a reason for each ranking.

It Won't Happen to Me

Tanya doesn't want to believe what the doctor at the clinic said— Tanya is two months pregnant. For the past two weeks, she had tried to convince herself otherwise. She had always believed it would never happen to her. She can pretend no longer. What is she going to do? Should she run away, convince her boyfriend to marry her, or get an abortion? Tanya wonders how she is going to tell her parents.

The doctor at the clinic gave her information about abortion. It doesn't seem all that bad. Still, she isn't sure. She had never really thought about abortion before. Tanya isn't sure about her beliefs. Father Whitman once said something about abortion being a sin. A friend's mother once said that she believes that a woman has the right to do what she wants because it is her body. As these thoughts race through Tanya's mind, the thought of facing her parents makes her cry. How can she tell them? They will be so disappointed. She again begins to think of running away.

Tanya decides to tell John, her boyfriend, first. They meet before school at their usual spot in front of the cafeteria. Tanya breaks the news to him quickly. John tells Tanya how much he loves her and will love their baby. He also tells her that if they were to marry, he couldn't finish high school and wouldn't be able to take advantage of the scholarship that has been awarded to him by the local university. He says that all his dreams and hopes of becoming an engineer would be gone if they were to marry. John goes to class, leaving Tanya alone and afraid.

At home that evening, Tanya tells her parents. Her father cannot believe that she could do this to them. He is furious. He worries about what their friends will think and asks how Tanya could embarrass the family like this, especially after all they have done for her. Tanya's parents believe that abortion is murder. They decide to send her to live with an aunt in another state. The baby will be put with an adoption agency when it is born. Tanya and her parents argue. They maintain that Tanya follow their plan. Tanya is confused and afraid. She has no idea what to do.

Two days later, an old boyfriend named Ryan calls Tanya. Ryan graduated a year early from school and is now in the marines. In desperation, Tanya tells him her story. Ryan says that he would marry her and would be a good father to the child. Tanya is stunned. What should she do? Everything is happening too fast. She decides to get an abortion even though she is unsure about her beliefs.

▪ Rank the responses of the following characters from best to worst: Tanya, the doctor, John, Tanya's parents, Ryan.
▪ Provide a reason for each ranking.

Double Trouble

Lou is tired of double dating. He cannot understand why Melinda's parents are so strict. They feel that Melinda shouldn't date alone until she is seventeen years old. Lou thinks that that is a little ridiculous. It is hard to find a couple willing to join them every time he and Melinda want to go somewhere. Walt tells Lou to tell Melinda's parents that Lou and Melinda will be double dating with him and his girlfriend, JoAnne. Walt and JoAnne plan to show up at Melinda's home with Lou to pick up Melinda; then the couples will go their separate ways. Walt assures Lou that nothing will go wrong. Lou thinks the idea will work, but he forgets to tell Melinda about it until he picks her up.

Melinda is angry as she gets into Lou's car. After she says hello to Walt and JoAnne, she calms down. She decides it is all right to pretend that she and Lou are double dating because she didn't know about the arrangement beforehand. She figures if something goes wrong, it won't be her fault. She decides to relax and enjoy the evening.

Later that evening, Melinda's mother calls Walt's mother, who is one of her best friends. During the conversation, she discovers, to her surprise, that Walt and JoAnne are there watching television. She had trusted Melinda, and she cannot believe what her daughter has done.

- Rank the actions of the following characters from best to worst: Lou, Melinda, Melinda's mother, Walt, JoAnne.
- Provide a reason for each ranking.

Only This Once

Rick has been cheating in math class for the past several weeks. He has been nominated for the "Most Outstanding Senior" award, and he needs a good grade in math in order to receive it. Basketball practice has been taking up much of his time, and next week is the last game. If the team wins, it will bring home the state championship. After the season, Rick knows he can start studying for math class again. He only has to cheat on one more test. He promises himself that he will study hard when basketball season is over. Rick reasons that the state championship is just as important as math class. He knows that he can do the math, and he is not cheating because he is stupid. Rick also knows that he must do well in basketball to ensure a spot on a college team. Rick needs a basketball scholarship to attend college, so he decides to cheat on just one more test.

Duke is Rick's closest friend. Rick has been copying from Duke's math test papers. Duke hasn't said much to Rick about cheating because he knows how much basketball means to Rick.

The other students in the class don't seem to mind if Rick cheats. They know he could do the work if he only had the time. The students want their school to be the state basketball champion. The students feel that it is Rick's business if he wants to cheat.

Rick tells Duke that he only needs to copy one more time. Duke is annoyed and tells Rick to study instead of copying. Rick reminds Duke of their friendship and tells Duke that he understands the math problems but that basketball is taking up all his study time. Duke finally gives in.

Duke's parents don't like Rick. In fact, they don't like any of Duke's friends at school. They want Duke to be more involved with the church youth group. Duke's father overhears Duke talking to Rick on the phone about cheating, and he angrily forbids Duke to talk to Rick again. Duke's parents will not listen to his side of the story. His mother can't understand why he doesn't have nicer friends. Duke's father believes he should tell the teacher that Rick has been cheating.

Duke decides he cannot let Rick cheat again even though he promised to help him. Duke also knows that he cannot tell the teacher about Rick. On the day of the test, Duke decides he will not purposely help Rick. If Rick happens to see Duke's test paper and cheats, it will not be his responsibility.

- Rank the actions of the following characters from best to worst: Rick, Duke, the students in class, Duke's father, Duke's mother.
- Provide a reason for each ranking.

Keep It to Yourself

Chuck does not have enough money to buy the new sound system he really wants. Chuck's mother agrees with Chuck's reasons for wanting to buy it. Chuck says that he wants to listen to "good" music but that there isn't much of it on the radio.

One afternoon, Bob, a friend of Chuck's, stops by the house. When Chuck explains his dilemma, Bob's eyes light up. He has a friend who has several sound systems that he is selling—and they are cheap. The two boys go to look at them. Chuck cannot decide whether to buy one or not. He tells Bob's friend that he will be back later. When Chuck is alone again with Bob, he asks Bob where he thinks his friend really got the sound systems. Bob says it is best not to ask questions. "What you don't know won't hurt you," is Bob's philosophy.

Chuck goes to his mom for advice. He explains that he really wants a sound system, but cannot afford to buy a new one. He tells her that Bob's friend has a system that would be perfect and that it is affordable. Chuck's mother tells him to do what he believes is best.

Chuck decides to buy the system from Bob's friend. It sounds great, and Bob believes that he did the right thing.

To earn some money to buy tapes, Chuck gets odd jobs around the neighborhood. One day, while cleaning a neighbor's garage, Chuck overhears a phone conversation. Apparently, the neighbor was robbed the night before, and the thief took his stereo and television. When the neighbor hangs up, he tells Chuck about the robbery. The police told the neighbor that robberies of this sort had been going on for the past several months. The police had not been able to catch the thief. The neighbor asks Chuck if he has any clues about the robberies. Chuck doesn't know how to respond. He finally decides that Bob is right—"What you don't know won't hurt you." Chuck says nothing and keeps the stereo.

■ Rank the actions of the following characters from best to worst: Chuck, Chuck's mother, Bob, Bob's friend.
■ Provide a reason for each ranking.

Fight for Your Rights

George is tired of being made fun of and tired of people laughing at him. He is tired of one person in particular—Jason. George is a member of the school's marching band. The old band uniform consists of oversized scratchy wool pants with shiny seats, a long coat with old-fashioned trim, and a hat that makes George look like a policeman.

George usually avoids trouble in general and Jason in particular, but today is different. The band is performing at a pep rally, and Jason has already cornered George in the locker room while George is putting on his uniform. Jason has a locker-room audience, and he isn't about to let the opportunity go to waste. George decides to ignore Jason, but he keeps up a barrage of insulting remarks. This doesn't

bother George until Jason shoves him, and that is the last straw.
George and Jason agree to a fight after the football game on Friday.

Later that evening, after a youth group meeting, George talks to
the youth minister about his trouble with Jason. The youth minister
advises George to avoid the fight and work toward a nonviolent way
of dealing with Jason. Then the youth minister says that everything
would work together for good for those who loved God. Because
things are not working together so well, George begins to question
God.

George's dad wants his son to defend himself. He believes George
has the right to fight and that George has his pride and dignity to
protect. He encourages George to take on Jason.

- Rank the actions of the following characters from best to worst:
  George, Jason, the youth minister, George's dad, the locker-room
  audience.
- Provide a reason for each ranking.

Is Marriage Forever?

Benita is out with her friends, leaving Jonathan home alone again. It
is the same story almost every night. Benita goes out drinking with
her friends and never spends any time at home. Tonight, however, is
different. Jonathan has decided to divorce Benita. He thinks that their
marriage is dead and that they have nothing in common.

Jonathan's parents were against the marriage from the start. They
told him not to marry right out of high school, and they never liked
Benita. They support Jonathan's decision to divorce Benita.

Jonathan had been confused about whether to get a divorce.
Father Alexis advised Jonathan to try to reason with Benita. However,
Jonathan began seeing a marriage counselor after Benita's drinking
worsened, and the counselor urged him to divorce Benita. She usually
isn't too bad, but sometimes she mistreats or neglects the children.
This is one of the main reasons for Jonathan's decision to divorce
Benita.

- Rank the decisions of the following characters from best to worst:
  Jonathan, Benita, Jonathan's parents, Father Alexis, the counselor.
- Provide a reason for each ranking.

Is It Worth It?

"It will strengthen your relationship." That is the advice Lori gives
to Teresa. Lori says she speaks from experience. She strongly recommends having sex as a way to secure Teresa's relationship with her
boyfriend. Teresa knows that if she doesn't have sex with Mark, they
will break up soon. She is confused and isn't sure what to do.

Mark and Teresa have been going steady for nearly a year, and
Mark has even mentioned to Andy that he might marry Teresa some-

day. They are serious, but they are not having sex. Andy cannot understand it.

Teresa makes her decision. After having sex with Mark, she writes three pages in her diary about their new relationship. Teresa decides that Lori was right. Having sex with Mark has brought them closer together.

Teresa's mother is furious! She found Teresa's diary while cleaning Teresa's room and read it. Teresa's mother tells her never to see Mark again.

- Rank the actions of the following characters from best to worst: Lori, Teresa, Mark, Andy, Teresa's mother.
- Provide a reason for each ranking.

The Forgotten Birthday

As Scott brushes his teeth, he thinks about how boring Fridays are. However, today would be different. Today is his sixteenth birthday. His mother is late for work, and as she rushes out the door, she reminds him to catch his bus on time. He is disappointed that his mom didn't remember his birthday, but he guesses it is because she is late for work.

Scott misses the bus again and has to walk to school. When he arrives, he realizes that he has missed his first period math test. He explains to the teacher, Mr. Russell, that he missed the bus. Mr. Russell does not care to hear his excuse. Scott cannot make up the test, so he flunks it.

Second period is no better than first. Megan, who sits next to Scott, asks him if he is going to Peter's party that evening. When Scott tells her he had not been invited, Megan says that everyone she knew had been invited.

Scott happens to see Peter in the cafeteria at lunch and he invites Scott to his party. Peter usually never talks to Scott except when he needs help in chemistry class, so Scott feels good about being invited to the party. However, he doesn't know whether to go or not. Peter said there would be plenty of beer and that his parents would be gone. Scott knows that his mother would never allow him to go to that kind of party.

When Scott arrives home that afternoon, his mother calls to say she would be working late. She says nothing about his birthday. That does it! Scott decides to go to the party. He cannot stand the thought of sitting at home another Friday evening alone.

- Rank the actions of the following characters from best to worst: Scott, Scott's mother, Mr. Russell, Megan, Peter.
- Provide a reason for each ranking.

Making Ends Meet

Every year when the parish council discusses the next year's budget, Father Harvey asks for a substantial increase. He argues that the parish needs the extra money to make the high payments to renovate something in the church. He also asks the council to allocate a sizable amount of money to an inner-city parish. Father believes the church has been neglecting the poor people.

The church treasurer is concerned with the rise in the cost of living. She thinks that a budget increase would force the congregation to reduce its standard of living or cause it to respond negatively.

If additional money is spent on the buildings and on the inner-city parish, the council would have to cut out the youth program, part of the religious education program, and the music budget. The council decides that it has to set priorities. "We must think of ourselves and our families first," Mrs. Ross tells the council. She will vote against Father Harvey's proposal.

Mr. Flarrity believes that things should be left the way they are. He feels that nothing is wrong with leaving things the way they are.

Mr. Sutter sees no need to fund the inner-city parish. He argues that the church has funded similar types of inner-city parishes in the past and that the bishop should just close them. He adds that if the poor people would get off welfare and start working, they would be better off and there would be no need to support them.

Mrs. Roberts argues that God's money should definitely be given to the inner city and not to church buildings.

- Rank the reactions of the following characters from best to worst: Father Harvey, the church treasurer, Mrs. Ross, Mr. Flarrity, Mr. Sutter, Mrs. Roberts.
- Provide a reason for each ranking.

Who Cares?

John resigns shortly after Nate's suicide. John was the youth minister at Immaculate Heart Church, but he had been thinking about leaving for six months. Shortly after Nate's suicide, John is offered a position in another town, and he jumps at the chance. He first considered leaving Immaculate Heart when he became aware of the attitude of the parish's youth group. They didn't care, and John felt that he could never count on them. They would commit themselves to an activity and then not show up. When a new person came to the parish youth activities, he or she was never welcomed.

Nate came to the group only a few months ago. John tried to help him with his problems, but the youth group offered little support. Nate was searching, but the group did not seem to care. Now it is too late.

An adult volunteer, Mrs. Wilson, chastises the group for at least an hour about their poor attitudes. She says she feels the suicide might have never occurred if the group had been more accepting of Nate.

She says that if the group had developed a relationship with Nate, he might still be alive today.

Over the next several weeks, a couple of the kids leave the group. A new youth director is found who is excited about the challenge of youth ministry. Soon Nate is forgotten.

- Rank the actions of the following characters from best to worst: John, Mrs. Wilson, the youth group, the few kids who leave the group.
- Provide a reason for each ranking.

The Food Store Robbery

The automobile company at which Ed has worked for the past ten years is experiencing hard times because of a recession and is forced to lay off employees. Management has left this responsibility to each of the plant managers. Ed's plant manager has been protecting his job for a long time and has always been worried that Ed might get his job. He lays off Ed to remove this threat.

Ed cannot find a job anywhere. After eighteen months of unsuccessful job hunting, his unemployment compensation runs out. Ed is forced to sell his insurance so his family can have food and make the house payments. When that money runs out, Ed and his wife, Hilda, discuss the possibility of applying for welfare. But he refuses to do so because he considers it too degrading and a sign of failure. Hilda urges Ed to reconsider; she offers to take a second job to help with the bills, although she knows an unskilled job will not bring in enough money.

One evening their child Timothy is playing in the street. A stolen car driven by a nineteen-year-old runaway hits and seriously injures Timothy. He requires hospitalization, and the bills mount. The driver does not have any insurance or money.

In desperation, Ed goes to the bank to apply for a loan, but the banker refuses the loan.

Distraught and confused, Ed robs the local food store. When Hilda returns, he lies to her about where the money came from, saying that a close friend loaned it to them. They use the money to buy food and clothing for the children. Within a day, Ed is arrested by the police. He explains, "All I wanted to do was feed my family."

After discussions with the city officials, the prosecutor decides to drop the case if Ed will pay back the money and seek counseling with the welfare department. But the store owner is a strong law-and-order advocate and refuses to drop the charges. He believes that Ed is a thief and ought to be punished. Ed is forced to go to trial where he pleads guilty and is sentenced by the judge.

- Who was most responsible for the robbery of the food store? Rank the characters from most responsible to least responsible: Ed, Ed's plant manager, Hilda, the runaway, the banker, city officials, the store owner.
- Provide a reason for each ranking.

The Party and the Practical Joke

Jimbo wants to go to a party at a friend's house. Everybody is going, and it looks like it will be a lot of fun. But on the same night, Jimbo's parents have decided to go out themselves, and they want Jimbo to stay home and babysit his little sister, Frieda, who is four years old. Frieda hates babysitters and won't stay home with any babysitter except Jimbo. Jimbo asks his parents if they could go out the following night instead, but they don't want to have to change their plans.

Jimbo doesn't like it, but he finally agrees to stay home with Frieda. Then Jimbo's friend Gregory calls and tells him that he is crazy. He talks Jimbo into going to the party for a little while. Gregory suggests that he wait until Frieda goes to sleep. Jimbo can then slip out of the house for fifteen minutes or so. Jimbo thinks that Gregory has a pretty good idea, so that is what he does.

At the party, a boy named Reggie—a real practical joker—sees Jimbo's car outside and decides to have a little fun. On the sly, he steals a small part out of Jimbo's engine and puts it in Jimbo's glove compartment. After about fifteen minutes, Jimbo gets in his car and tries to leave, but the car won't start. He discovers the "practical joke," but he can't figure out who did it, and he cannot find the part. Over thirty minutes have passed, so time is now becoming important.

Jimbo asks his friend Skipper for a ride, but Skipper is busy talking to the prettiest girl in school, and he doesn't want to be bothered. Jimbo considers asking Lucy, but she has been drinking a lot of beer and smoking some marijuana. She can barely stand up—let alone drive a car.

Reggie finally decides he has had enough fun, so he tells Jimbo where the missing part is. Jimbo doesn't think it is very funny, so he punches Reggie, knocking him to the floor and cutting his lip.

When Jimbo finally gets home, he discovers that Frieda has awakened and has been screaming and crying. The next-door neighbors have come over to find out what is going on. Jimbo asks them to please not tell his folks what happened. But they tell Jimbo that they feel it is their duty to inform his parents of the incident.

- Rank the actions of the following characters from best to worst: Jimbo, his parents, Frieda, Gregory, Reggie, Skipper, Lucy, the neighbors.
- Provide a reason for each ranking.

The Two-timer

Barry had been going steady with Linda for two years, but he is beginning to feel that their relationship is turning into a habit. They check with one another about every little thing. Still, Linda is great to be with. She is attractive and bright. Barry knows that if they break up, there would be a line of guys at Linda's door.

Don, Barry's best friend, wouldn't mind going with Linda, but as long as she is Barry's girlfriend, he decides she is off-limits. So Don is caught off guard when Barry tells him he has a date with a girl named Lisa.

Don is angry. "But what about Linda? Are you going to break up with her?"

Barry looks surprised. "Heck no, Don, at least not for a while. I still care a lot about Linda, and I'm not sure about Lisa yet. Besides, I don't want to hurt Linda's feelings." Now Don is really upset. His best friend is two-timing Linda, and he feels that it is not right.

Linda confronts Barry right after school. "I can't believe you would do this to me, Barry. I thought you cared about me, but then I find out you have been dating some other girl."

Barry feels panicky. For the first time in the two years they have been going together, Barry realizes how much he cares about Linda. "Okay, Linda. I did go out with Lisa once, but that's all. I'm sorry. Please give me another chance."

Then Linda stops, looks straight at Barry, and says, "I wondered if you would tell me the truth. You did. So I guess I can tell you the truth. I've dated another guy a couple of times myself. I thought I was getting tired of you, but when Don told me you were cheating, I realized how much I loved you. So maybe this experience has been good for both of us."

Now it is Barry's turn to be shocked. He just stands there. He is angry at Don for betraying him and at Linda for cheating on him and for setting him up. He looks at Linda coldly. "Now I know who I can trust—and it isn't you or Don. Maybe you two ought to get together. You deserve each other. See you around."

When Barry arrives home, he calls Don to tell him their friendship is over. Then he calls Lisa to see how things are looking for the weekend.

■ Rank the actions of the following characters from best to worst: Barry, Don, Linda, Lisa.

■ Provide a reason for each ranking.

It Happened So Fast

Jessica is just one of those helpful, likable people. She is always cheerful and available when you need her. She is active in 4-H Club, the school senate, and the drill team, and she is a leader in the youth group at Assumption. Because of her responsibilities, Jessica is busy with activities almost every night of the week.

But the last few days have been terrible. Jessica had to work the entire weekend at her house. Her father had taken his yearly hunting trip, so Jessica had to stay home and help her mom with cleaning before the holidays. Jessica was up late every night during the past week, and after working the entire weekend, she is exhausted. If that isn't bad enough, her boyfriend, Tom, calls on Sunday and is mad because Jessica hasn't spent any time with him. She promises to see him Monday night. After she hangs up, she remembers she has a youth group meeting at Assumption that night, and Mary Beth, a youth minister, told her that her attendance is vital. Jessica decides to go but to leave early.

Just before Jessica leaves for the meeting on Monday night, her mother gives her a lecture about being gone too much and tells her to be home before 9:00 p.m. That is okay with Jessica, because she plans to see Tom at 8:00 p.m.

Everyone else is late for the meeting, so it doesn't start until 7:10. The meeting runs overtime, so Jessica tells the group she has to leave. Mary Beth objects and presses Jessica to stay. Jessica stays, but all she can think about is Tom and her parents waiting for her.

The meeting finally ends at 8:40. Jessica jumps in her car and rushes home. As she races around Donner's Point, a deer jumps in front of the car. She slams on the brakes, and the car goes out of control. Jessica is not wearing a seat belt. She is thrown from the car and is killed instantly. The police say that if she had been observing the speed limit, it is likely she would have received only minor-to-moderate injuries.

- Rank the actions of the following characters from best to worst: Jessica, Tom, her father, her mother, Mary Beth, the young people who were late for the meeting.
- Provide a reason for each ranking.

Hard Choices

After Heather graduated from high school and junior college, she became a legal secretary for a local law firm. She married her high school sweetheart, Jerry, who is now a supermarket manager.

She has been experiencing pain in her armpit. At first she thinks the worst—cancer. She immediately arranges to see Dr. Hadley, the family physician. He checks her and assures her there is nothing to worry about. He diagnoses an infection that requires antibiotics.

A year passes, but the soreness never goes away. In addition, Heather is almost sure she is pregnant, so she decides to see a gynecologist, who confirms that she is indeed pregnant. She tells the doctor about the pain under her arm, and the doctor is concerned. She sends Heather to a specialist who diagnoses breast cancer. The specialist says that the tumor has grown considerably and that the pregnancy will prevent proper treatment.

The specialist, Dr. Williams, recommends that the baby be aborted immediately and that a radical mastectomy (removal of the breast, the nodes, and the pectoral muscles) be performed at once and be followed by radiation and chemotherapy.

Heather seeks three other medical opinions, but the recommendations are exactly the same: Abort the baby and have the surgery.

Heather and Jerry talk over the options carefully. Jerry wants Heather to abort the baby and follow the doctors' instructions. Heather wants to have the baby. Jerry reluctantly agrees. The doctors strenuously argue that surgery and radiation treatment could seriously harm the baby, so she decides to wait until after the baby is born before having her cancer treated. All the doctors, Heather's family, her husband, *everyone,* disagrees with her decision. But Heather wants the baby, and she will not allow it to be aborted.

Six months later, Heather's baby is born with a serious birth defect, possibly caused by the antibiotics that Heather took early in her pregnancy. In due time, Heather has the surgery and the therapy. She gives up her job to stay home with her baby.

Jerry never does accept their baby. He cannot forgive Heather for risking her life and possibly leaving him with the child to raise alone. Eventually, he files for divorce.

Heather's cancer is now in remission, but the doctors cannot say when or if it will return.

■ Rank the actions of the following characters from best to worst: Heather, Jerry, Dr. Hadley, Dr. Williams.

■ Provide a reason for each ranking.

The Last to Know

Ever since Lee overheard his parents talking about Stan's parents, he has been dying to find out if what they said was true. "Hey, Stan, my folks said your parents had to get married because your mom was pregnant with you. That's not true, is it?" Lee can tell by the look on Stan's face that he never should have said anything. Stan does not reply. He does not have to. It is obvious that he knew nothing.

When Stan gets home, he storms downstairs to confront his mother. "Mom, did you and Dad have to get married? Were you pregnant with me? I want to know the truth, Mom."

Lana feels that she has no choice. She and her husband, Rob, have discussed this many times. Rob thinks that Stan should never know. Lana disagrees and cannot keep quiet any longer. "Stan, I've wanted to tell you for a long time, but we just didn't know how or when to tell you. Yes, it's true."

Stan does not respond. He just sits there, looking out the window. Finally, he says, "Mom, have you and Dad been talking about getting a divorce?"

Lana is caught off guard again. "Well, Stan, we have been talking about it, yes."

Stan stands up. "I thought so. I knew you and Dad were unhappy. Now I know why. It's me. You should have never gotten married!" Stan says he wants to be alone and goes to his room.

Lana doesn't know what to do. She is afraid to tell Rob, but knows she must. When Rob comes home, she tells him what happened. He explodes, "How could you do that? Now you've made it impossible for me to have any kind of relationship with him. I'll never be able to look him in the eye! Didn't you stop to think what this would do to Stan? Why couldn't you have denied it?"

Rob goes up to Stan's room and knocks on the door. There is no answer. He goes inside. The room is very neat, but Stan is gone. All Rob finds is a note. Stan has run away from home.

■ Rank the decisions of the following characters from best to worst:

Stan, Lana, Rob, Lee, Lee's parents.

■ Provide a reason for each ranking.

No Place to Go

Fourteen-year-old Sheila has no place to go. Her father has been having a sexual relationship with her since she was nine. At first, she was frightened, but her father said he loved her and that it was normal for a father to express his love. She loved him too and didn't want to hurt him. As Sheila got older, she realized that something was very wrong. Her father has warned her not to tell anyone, and she hasn't. But she cannot keep it to herself any longer. Sheila feels guilty that she did not stop this a long time ago. She feels responsible for what has happened.

Something else bothers her as well. A number of times, Sheila's mother has seen him leaving her room. Sheila wonders if her mom knows.

Sheila decides to talk to the priest. Sheila nervously tells Father McKinley her problem. She is not prepared for his response. He tries to suggest that maybe Sheila was fantasizing or that maybe she misunderstood what her father was doing. Father McKinley reminds Sheila that her father is a good man. He tells Sheila to pray.

In desperation, Sheila decides to tell her boyfriend. She believes Mike will understand. But he just looks at her with disgust. He says, "Come on, Sheila, with your father? This has been going on for five years? That makes me sick. Why didn't you tell somebody? Why didn't you do something about it before now?" Sheila can tell that Mike is genuinely shaken up. When she doesn't hear from him for the next few days, she knows their relationship is finished. Sheila really feels alone now. She has to do something. She decides to risk talking to her mother.

Sheila waits until her father has left for work and then asks her mom to sit down. Sheila forces the truth out. Her mother begins yelling and crying and threatening all at the same time. She tells Sheila never to bring up the subject again. She tells Sheila she is wrong to accuse her father of such a horrible act. Sheila is crushed. She believes that her mother has known the truth all along but is afraid to admit it.

Sheila feels bitter, alone, and depressed. She goes to the medicine cabinet and takes out her mother's bottle of sleeping pills. She locks her bedroom door and swallows the entire bottleful. As she becomes more and more drowsy, she keeps asking herself why no one was willing or able to help her.

■ Who is most responsible for Sheila's suicide attempt? Rank the actions of the characters in order from most responsible to least responsible: Sheila's dad, Sheila's mom, Sheila, Mike, Father McKinley.

■ Provide a reason for each ranking.

Stepwitch

"Marci, I want that room cleaned up before you go, or you will be grounded again. Is that clear?"

Marci's stepmother is at it again. Sometimes Marci feels as though her stepmother hates her. She is always yelling at Marci about something. If it's not her room, it is her hair or her makeup or her bathroom or the stereo. Marci really cannot understand what her dad sees in her.

When Marci first asked her father if she could go live with her mom, her father had said she was overreacting. "Look, Marci," he said, "Jan has treated you very well. She just wants you to clean up after yourself and abide by some rules. Any mother would expect the same thing." Marci doesn't agree. She knows lots of girls who don't have to clean up their rooms or dress a certain way. She feels that all these rules are stupid.

Although Marci is old enough to decide if she wants to live with her mom, she loves her dad very much. Marci decides to tell him that she is thinking about living with her mother. "You can, Marci, if that's what you really want. I can't stop you. I do want you to understand one thing. Once you move, that is it. You can't move in with your mother for a month, decide you don't like the arrangement, and then move back with us."

Marci tries to talk with her stepmother once more to see if they can work things out. Jan responds, "Marci, I am not trying to make your life miserable. I love you as if you were my own daughter. I understand how difficult it must be to have a stepmother and to do things the way I want them done. But if you decide to stay here, I will expect you to live by the rules."

That makes Marci angry. "How can Jan understand? Jan doesn't know what it is like to have two mothers," Marci says to herself, "and she sure doesn't know what it was like before Dad remarried. Before Jan came along, it was just him and me. He never cared whether I cleaned up my room. We got along great until the stepwitch arrived." Marci makes up her mind. She is going to live with her mom.

- Rank the actions of the following characters from best to worst: Marci, Jan, Marci's dad.
- Provide a reason for each ranking.

The Dud Youth Worker

Everyone in the youth group at Holy Trinity is stunned. Sandy has been their youth minister for the last three years. She is sensitive, funny, and a great athlete. The attendance at the youth group has grown from seventeen to about seventy. Sometimes, at special meetings, as many as two hundred young people show up. Something neat is always going on. Now Sandy is leaving to enter a religious community. She says that it was a tough decision, but she feels sure this is what she truly wants to do. She assures the youth group that the church will make sure the youth program continues just like it is now.

Then Charles shows up to be the youth minister. He looks like a real mess, and he is no fun. There are so many Charles jokes floating around that no one can even say his name with a straight face.

"This is ridiculous," complains Ken, a leader of the group. "There won't be any kids left in our youth group if we don't get rid of this dork." The kids try to call Sandy, but she has already gone and hasn't even left a forwarding number.

The leaders of the youth group go to see Father Frank. They try to get him to understand that the youth program is going to disintegrate unless they get rid of Charles. Father says he understands their concern but has full confidence in Charles. The kids leave the meeting frustrated. They decide to give Charles three more weeks, and if things don't get better, they will tell their parents that they are finished with the youth group until Charles leaves.

Everyone agrees with that except Teresa. Teresa is a loner. She says that the kids shouldn't be going to the youth group because of the youth minister; they should be going to learn about God. She tries to convince everyone that even if Charles isn't as cool as Sandy, maybe he knows God as well as Sandy does. The rest of the group ignores Teresa's arguments. They point out that there won't be anyone left to learn about God if none of the kids want to come.

Charles does not get any better, and eventually, a lot of the kids quit coming, but Teresa hangs in there. Suddenly, just six months after he became the youth minister, Charles quits. By this time, only seven kids are attending the youth group, and they only meet twice a month. The youth group is a shambles, and Teresa is disillusioned.

- Rank the decisions of the following characters from best to worst: Sandy, Ken, Teresa, Father Frank, Charles.
- Provide a reason for each ranking.

Nobody Will Know

How can she be pregnant? Tess broke up with Norm a month ago, and they had made only one mistake. What a mistake it is turning out to be!

Tess is active in her youth group. She is deeply committed to her faith. So are her parents. They had warned her not to get too involved with Norm. Gary, the youth minister, had warned her, too. It seems like everyone had warned her. Tess had prayed really hard that she would not get pregnant, but all her praying didn't help.

Tess decides to confide in her best friend, Barbie, who tells Tess to get an abortion. "Your parents will never know, Tess. No one will know." Tess does not believe in abortion, but she thinks that if she has this baby it will ruin her life, her parents' lives, and Norm's life. Barbie encourages her, "Tess, it's the only way. It's easy, and no one gets hurt." Tess decides to go ahead with the abortion.

"What's this?" Tess's mom is standing over her. Her father is right behind her mom. Tess's mom is holding a business card from the Youth Care Pregnancy Counseling Center. "Tess, are you pregnant? What is going on?"

Tess is frightened. "Where did you get that, Mom? Did you go rummaging through my purse again?"

"It doesn't matter where or how I got this, Tess. I want to know what is going on."

"Okay, Mother, okay. No, I'm not pregnant, but I did get an abortion. I'm okay, so don't worry."

Tess's mother is shocked. Her father just stares at her. She can tell he is hurt and disappointed.

Tess cannot hold it back any longer. She thought that she could get through it alone, but now she realizes she can't. Tess looks at her mother and father. "Mom and Dad, I lied. I mean, I *am* pregnant, but I didn't get an abortion. I was going to—that's why I have the business card—but I haven't gone yet."

She is not prepared for her parents' response. They sit there talking as though she isn't even present. They are discussing all the options, *including* abortion. Tess is horrified that her parents could actually consider her getting an abortion when they had always taught her it is wrong.

Finally, they say, "Tess, based on the fact that you are so young, and there is so much at stake, we think you should go ahead with the abortion."

Tess cannot believe what she is hearing. Her parents were suggesting an abortion. "So," Tess says bitterly, "abortion is wrong for everyone else, I guess, unless it's your own daughter?"

Tess's mother speaks softly now, "That's not true, Tess. We still believe abortion is wrong, but sometimes there can be things more wrong than abortion."

Tess stands up. "Yeah, Mom, I see what you mean. What is more wrong than abortion is having your friends find out that your wonderful daughter is pregnant. That's what's really wrong, isn't it?"

■ Rank the actions and the decisions of the following characters from best to worst: Tess, Norm, Barbie, Tess's mom, Tess's dad.

■ Provide a reason for each ranking.

The Double Cross

Laura and her boyfriend, Al, have been hassling over whether to have sex. Laura thinks intercourse before marriage is wrong. Al doesn't. Laura's best friend, Sally, and her boyfriend, Bob, have been having intercourse for over a year. Sally tells Laura she is crazy not to have sex with Al. Al gives Laura an ultimatum. He suggests that if Laura does not have sex with him, then she must not love him. Laura still says no, so Al breaks up with her.

Laura is upset about Al's breaking up with her. One night while out at a shopping center, Laura runs into Bob, Sally's boyfriend. Bob seems concerned about her, so Laura agrees to go out for a soda and to talk. Bob is understanding and before Laura knows what is happening, she and Bob are kissing. Laura knows she shouldn't do this, but it feels so good to be with Bob now that Al has left her. Somehow they end up at the beach and before the night is over, they have sex.

Laura doesn't hear from Bob again, but about a week after the beach incident, Sally comes to Laura devastated. She confides that she has herpes and that she got it from Bob. "Did you know that Bob is sleeping around with a bunch of other girls?" Sally asks.

Laura tries not to worry. She had sex with Bob only once, but she has noticed that she has some sores on her genital area. She is frightened and decides to tell Sally about her one night with Bob. Sally just looks at Laura with disgust and starts laughing, "So you *did* have sex with Bob? I thought so. Some friend you are. Well, Laura, you can find someone else's shoulder to cry on. I *don't* have herpes. I just wanted to see who Bob is playing around with. Now I know. Thanks for being such a good Christian friend."

Sally then confronts Bob, who tells Sally that everything was Laura's fault. "Hey, she came on to me. I just couldn't help it. She got me all turned on and said it would really hurt her if I didn't. Honest."

When Al hears about Laura and Bob, he calls Laura up and tells her he would like to get back together. Laura agrees to go steady again.

- Rank the actions of the following characters from best to worst: Laura, Al, Sally, Bob.
- Provide a reason for each ranking.

Double Date—Double Trouble

Mark and Trevor, both juniors in high school, decide to go on a double date. Mark invites his girlfriend, Julie, and Trevor invites his girlfriend, Candice. Mark just got his driver's license, and the night of the double date is the first time he has been allowed to take the family car. Mark's father gives him only two rules: Be home on time and do not drive out of town.

Mark gets home from his date and says that everything went great. Mark's dad asks how Candice, who lives ten miles out of town, got home. Mark tells him that Trevor's parents took her home.

The next day, Mark and his father attend a high school basketball game together. Mark's dad sees Trevor and comments that he looks a little glum. Mark says that Trevor is grounded because he went out with Candice last night. It seems that Trevor has been restricted from dating Candice but went out with her anyway, without his parents' knowledge. Mark's dad thinks for a minute and then says, "But, Mark, if Trevor took Candice out last night without his parents' knowledge, who took Candice home?" Mark starts to say that Candice's parents came into town and picked her up, but realizes, in the middle of his sentence, that he has been caught. Mark's dad says, "You took Candice home, didn't you? You not only disobeyed my request that you not go out of town, but you lied to me, right?"

Mark looks a little pale, "Yes, Dad."

"You're grounded, Mark, indefinitely! I just don't understand how you could lie to me the first time you're allowed the use of the car."

Mark explains that he didn't know that Trevor was restricted from dating Candice until he met them for the date, *and* he did not know that he had to take her home until then either.

Mark's dad says that all Mark had to do was to call and tell him the situation and that chances were he would have understood and allowed Mark to drive Candice home or would have taken her home himself.

■ Who is most responsible for Mark's restriction? Rank the characters in order from most responsible to least responsible: Mark, Trevor, Candice, Julie, Mark's father.

■ Provide a reason for each ranking.

Little Things Mean a Lot

Jon and Linda are active in their youth group. Their best friends are Ken and Sue. Ken is one of the leaders of the youth group. The two couples spend most of their weekends together at church activities or at school events.

During Christmas vacation, Jon, Linda, Ken, and Sue attend the church high school retreat. The speaker at the retreat speaks about living the Christian life in all areas. He points out that the seemingly little things such as lying, cheating, and disobeying your parents are important.

After they come back from the retreat Jon and Linda start having tension in their relationship. Linda doesn't want to write Jon's English papers any longer, and she won't let him look at her answers during the algebra exam. Jon becomes angry. He thinks Linda is being ridiculous, and he gets Ken and Sue to agree with him. They all talk to Linda after school one day. They point out that they are all moral people, that Linda and Jon are practically married, that they don't take drugs or drink, and that Linda shouldn't get upset about little things that don't matter.

Linda is hurt. She is angry with Jon for turning Ken and Sue against her. After thinking about it for a day, she breaks up with Jon. That weekend Jon goes out and gets drunk with a bunch of friends. He tells them that Linda is a religious phony and a sleaze.

When Linda hears about what Jon said, she is upset. She goes to the youth minister and asks him if she did the right thing. The youth minister encourages Linda and tells her that in the long run her friends will respect her. He feels sure that she will be able to count on her friends to be there for support.

That night when Linda attends the group, Ken and Sue won't talk to her. Linda begins to wonder if what the youth minister said was really true.

- Rank the actions and the decisions of the following characters from best to worst: Linda, Jon, Ken, Sue, the youth minister.
- Provide a reason for each ranking.

The Champagne Dinner

Kirk and Anna have been going together for over a year. Kirk is a senior in high school, and Anna is a junior. Recently, since Kirk found out that his parents were going to get a divorce, he has been upset. As a result, he and Anna have become more sexually intimate. Anna has resisted intercourse because she feels that it is wrong. However, because Kirk has been so torn up over his parents, she has been finding it harder and harder to say no.

Harold and Denise are Kirk and Anna's best friends. They, too, have been going together for over a year. They have attended many church-sponsored camps and retreats together, and they have decided they are going to be married. Harold and Denise have an active sex life, and they see no contradiction between their sexual involvement and their faith. They argue that they take precautions and that they plan on getting married.

During Easter break, Kirk, Anna, Harold, and Denise spend the day at the beach. At the end of the day, as they drive home, they decide to stop at a restaurant. They have such a good time at dinner that Kirk suggests buying some champagne and having a little celebration. Anna is reluctant, but the rest of them argue that they won't get drunk on just one bottle.

After dropping Harold and Denise off, Kirk invites Anna into his house. His parents are gone for the weekend. Anna agrees. Before the night is over, Kirk and Anna have sexual intercourse.

The next day Anna feels terribly guilty. She feels like she has let down God, her parents, herself, and everyone. She also feels like a hypocrite. She confides all these feelings to Denise, but Denise doesn't understand. She reasons that Anna loves Kirk, and he is hurting right now, so Anna is being a comfort to him.

Anna doesn't feel any better. She goes to her parish's celebration of Reconciliation. Afterward, she recognizes that God forgives her and that even though she is sorry, she knows that her relationship with Kirk will be more difficult because it will be hard to keep from having sex again. Eventually, Anna breaks up with Kirk, even though she still cares a lot for him.

- Rank the actions of the following characters from best to worst: Kirk, Anna, Denise, Harold.
- Provide a reason for each ranking.

The Senior Prom

Stephanie and Darlene are both seniors. They are going to the prom with their boyfriends, Cliff and Roger. Stephanie and Darlene are active in their parish youth group. One day, their youth minister, Cy, tells the girls that the church has committed itself to sponsor a diocesan-wide party and dinner that is scheduled for the same night as the prom. Cy apologizes and says that the event has been scheduled for two years.

When Cy finds out that Stephanie, Darlene, Roger, and Cliff are all going to the prom, he asks them to stay after the youth group meeting and talk about it. He tells them that he needs them as parish leaders to set an example for the young people of the diocese. All four of them tell Cy that they are sorry but that they are still going to the prom. It is only four weeks away. The girls have already purchased their dresses, and the guys have reserved their tuxedos. They ask Cy why he hadn't told them earlier.

Both Stephanie and Darlene's parents strongly advise them to make their own decision.

■ Rank the decisions of the following characters from best to worst: Stephanie, Darlene, Roger, Cliff, Stephanie's parents, Darlene's parents, Cy.
■ Provide a reason for each ranking.

Who Killed Raoul?

Raoul is a tough kid. You have to be to survive in his country. This past year has been a nightmare for him. He and his parents have been one of the luckier families. They own a small piece of land that they are able to farm. It is hard work, but they are always able to provide enough food for their family and still have something for other families. Most months, they are even able to save a little money.

Then the nightmare starts. The government condemns their land. Government troops show up late one night and demand that they abandon their property because the government has sold it to a multinational corporation. Raoul's parents refuse, and they tell the government troops to leave. Then they meet with all the other land-owners and suggest that they form a protest movement.

Two weeks later, Raoul's sister disappears. Raoul's family knows that they will never see her again. Just one week later, Raoul's brother is found beaten so severely that he has permanent brain damage.

Raoul's family breaks. They decide to leave the country and try to find freedom from oppression. They collect all their savings and purchase illegal passage on a small boat to the United States. The boat is small and crowded and is guarded by three men with submachine guns. After they put out to sea, the gunmen take everyone's wallets, money, jewelry, and anything else that has value. Then a storm hits. Only ten of the thirty-three people survive, and Raoul is one of them.

When Raoul regains consciousness, he is in a U.S. detention camp. He learns about a large community of people from his country in New York. He and several others escape from the camp one night and make it to New York City.

Raoul finds a family to stay with for a while, but when it becomes obvious that he cannot find a job, the family asks him to leave. He begins to roam the streets and soon meets up with a gang who survives by committing muggings and small-time robberies. Eventually he decides to participate in a big-time robbery of a jewelry store. At first Raoul hesitates, but then he realizes that if his share of the money is enough, he will be able to get out of New York and make a legitimate start.

The night of the robbery something goes wrong. A silent alarm is tripped. When the gang comes out of the store, the police are waiting. The gang members begin to fire at the police and run. The police return fire, and Raoul is killed.

- Rank the actions and the decisions of the following characters from best to worst: Raoul, the government of Raoul's country, Raoul's parents, the multinational corporation that purchased Raoul's family's property.
- Provide a reason for each ranking.

Choosing Between Mom and Dad

Belinda's parents' divorce is final. No one except Belinda and her parents know that the real reason for the divorce is that her dad is a homosexual. Belinda feels sorry for her mom because she is deeply depressed over the whole thing.

Belinda has decided to stay with her mom after the divorce. Her dad *does* seem genuinely sorry about the divorce, and most important to Belinda, he told her that he still loves her very much. He wrote Belinda a beautiful letter in which he apologized for hurting both Belinda and her mother. In the letter, her father described his battle with homosexuality—a battle that had been going on since he was a little boy. He shared that he had sought help from a number of priests and finally accepted the fact that he could no longer fight his homosexuality.

One afternoon, about two months after the divorce, Belinda sees her mother and a strange man holding hands and talking intimately. She is crushed. All of a sudden, everything is upside down, and nothing makes sense anymore.

When Belinda comes home she calls her father and tells him what she saw. Her father encourages Belinda not to be so harsh on her mother, but Belinda cannot forgive her mother for cheating on her father.

Belinda makes up her mind to go stay with her father. After she packs, Belinda writes a note for her mother and leaves.

- Rank the following characters' actions and decisions from best to worst: Belinda, Belinda's mother, Belinda's father.
- Provide a reason for each ranking.

A Gift or a Curse?

Matt prays quietly after Mass. He has a problem with masturbation, and he feels ashamed and guilty. Matt has been masturbating regularly since he was twelve, and now he is sixteen. He knows that it is wrong, but when he masturbates he feels both good and bad at the same time. A book he read said that masturbation was a "gift from God," but Matt remembered his church's youth director saying that masturbation was a sin and not God's will. Matt tried to find something in the Bible related to his problem but couldn't find anything.

In desperation, Matt shares his problem with his best friend, Pete. Pete says that he masturbated a few times but that he didn't like it. Matt thinks about talking to a priest, but he thinks that he would just tell him to quit doing what he was doing and pray that God would take the desire away. Matt's older brother advises him to find a girlfriend.

- Rank the actions of the following characters from best to worst: Matt, Matt's older brother, Pete.
- Provide a reason for each ranking.

Like Mother, Like Daughter

Kirsten's mom is an alcoholic. She drinks at home during the day. In the evening, she stumbles through dinner and then falls asleep in front of the television.

Kirsten never knows what to expect from her. Sometimes her mom is angry and verbally abuses anyone in the same room. Other times, she is depressed. Then she tearfully apologizes to Kirsten and promises never to drink again. At times like this she promises to take Kirsten shopping the next day and buy her lots of new clothes. But the promises are never kept.

Kirsten doesn't know what to think of her dad either. Most of the time he is very understanding. He makes excuses for her mother. He never mentions her drinking problem to others. But it is strange: Every time Kirsten's mom *stops* drinking, he yells at her constantly, belittling her and calling her a loser and a bad mother, telling her about all the embarrassment and pain she has caused Kirsten and him. He complains about the lack of money and accuses her of drinking their happiness away. So Kirsten's mom starts drinking again, and he again becomes the perfect example of a loving and devoted husband.

Kirsten hates her mom's drinking, but she also hates the way her dad acts when her mom tries to stop drinking. Kirsten wonders sometimes whether her dad *wants* her mom to drink. She feels terrible for thinking such a thing, but she cannot rid herself of these thoughts. Kirsten and her dad never talk about her mom and her drinking. Once Kirsten suggested that they all go for counseling. Her dad had a fit and insisted that it was her mom who was sick, not them. Kirsten never brought it up again.

Kirsten goes to her school counselor, who tells her that alcoholism is a disease and that her mom needs understanding, love, and medical help. Kirsten goes to the youth minister at Saint Ansgar's. She agrees with the counselor but says that it would help if Kirsten would pray for her family.

Kirsten cares a lot for her father, but she has her own life to lead, too. Kirsten feels pretty lucky to have a boyfriend like Rick. He is always there when she needs him, and lately she needs him a lot. They are involved sexually, and that is because of Kirsten, not Rick. She needs the sexual closeness. For Kirsten, Rick is everything. She knows she loves him and that eventually they will get married. That's why she isn't prepared when one day at school Rick says the relationship is over. He says that he doesn't want to be so serious. He says he feels that for Kirsten sex is a drug to help her escape her problems and that he is tired of being used.

Kirsten is devastated. She didn't know people could hurt so much. She leaves school and runs home. No one is there. She is almost hysterical, and that frightens her. She doesn't know what to do. Then she considers doing something she thought she would never do. She finds some wine in the refrigerator and pours herself a glass. It goes down more easily than she thought. She does feel better. She has one more and then another. Kirsten's dad comes home at five. Kirsten is asleep on the couch and an empty bottle of wine is on the floor.

- Rank the actions and the decisions of the following characters from best to worst: Kirsten, her mom, her dad, the school counselor, the youth minister, Rick.
- Provide a reason for each ranking.

Close Call

It was a close call. Veronica and Denny have been going together for three years now, and both of them are still virgins. That could have ended tonight. Luckily, they were interrupted by another couple coming to the same spot.

Veronica is so upset that she cannot sleep. She really likes Denny a lot, and she can easily imagine marrying a guy like him. He is thoughtful, kind, intelligent, and he isn't pushy. Veronica believes that sex before marriage is wrong, and she believes that getting pregnant is worse. She doesn't believe in abortion, and the thought of having a baby in high school is more than she can handle.

Veronica decides to talk with her parents about what she should do. She has always been open with them. Veronica talks to her mom first: "Mom, I'm getting worried. Denny and I have been getting pretty serious and, well, you know, we've kind of been carried away sexually. We haven't done anything yet, so don't panic, but I'm afraid we might. Should I think about birth control, Mom?"

Veronica's mom tells Veronica that she and her husband trust Veronica and like Denny. However, Veronica's mother just cannot accept the idea of Veronica's using birth control pills.

Veronica's father suggests that she and Denny break up for a while to let things cool off. He says that if they really love each other, they can wait until they are both older. Veronica doesn't like that answer at all.

Donna, the youth minister, feels that using birth control is like planning to have sex. She says that it is just a myth that all couples have sex, and that lots of couples wait until marriage to have sex. Donna emphasizes that birth control is like acknowledging that sex is inevitable and that planning on having sex before marriage is condoning it.

But one afternoon after school, Denny and Veronica stop by her house to change clothes for a swim party, and suddenly they are in Veronica's bedroom having sex. Her parents are at work.

Denny panics. Tearful and apologetic, he tells Veronica that if she gets pregnant she will have to get an abortion. Veronica cannot believe it. Denny knows that she is against abortion. Veronica explains that she is on the pill. But that makes Denny more upset. He accuses Veronica of planning the whole afternoon. He cannot believe that she is on the pill. Veronica responds, "Well, it's a good thing I am on the pill, or I might have had to face pregnancy alone!"

Denny blurts out his response, "Veronica, if you lied about this, who knows what else you've been lying about! Maybe you've been on the pill a lot longer than I know. Maybe I'm not the only one—." He doesn't finish his sentence. He knows he went too far.

Through her tears, Veronica tells Denny to get out and never come back. He tries to apologize, but it is too late. He leaves. Neither of them officially breaks up. They just never see each other again.

- Rank the actions of the following characters from best to worst: Veronica, Denny, Veronica's mom, Veronica's dad, the youth minister.
- Provide a reason for each ranking.

The Search

Paul's mother is searching his room when she hears Paul at the front door. She had found a marijuana pipe hidden in the closet, but no pot. She had decided to search his room when she heard him talking to a friend on the phone about being wasted. She is shocked. She never dreamed this would happen to her son.

She goes out to meet Paul in the hallway, holding the pipe. Paul thinks, "How did Mother find out? Why can't she leave me alone and let me make my own decisions? I don't interfere with *her* life. I don't say anything to her about the wine she drinks at dinner. What gives her the right to tell *me* how to live? After all, I'm seventeen years old."

Paul's mom asks him what the "thing," as she calls it, was doing in his closet. She throws it against the wall; it breaks into a hundred pieces. Paul says nothing. He turns and walks into his room.

After a day of giving his mom the silent treatment, Paul decides to tell her the truth about the pipe. He says it really isn't his; he is keeping it for a friend. The two of them have been smoking a few bowls of pot on the weekends for about three months. His pot smoking is under control. He tells his mother that she has nothing to worry about. He explains that he smokes pot like she drinks wine. He isn't going to become drug dependent, just like she isn't going to become an alcoholic.

Paul's mom takes exception to this. She tells Paul that he has to see a drug counselor or move out of the house. Paul had thought that telling the truth would get him off the hook. So much for telling the truth, he concludes.

But Paul does see a drug counselor, who feels that Paul has a serious drug problem and that he is involved with more drugs than he has admitted to. The counselor recommends that Paul be placed in a residential drug treatment center. After listening to the advice of the counselor, Paul's mother tells Paul that if he refuses to enter the treatment center, he will have to move out of the house.

When Paul calls to explain his situation to his dad, he says that Paul should live with him. Paul decides to move in with his dad.

■ Rank the actions and the decisions of the following characters from best to worst: Paul, Paul's father, Paul's mother, the drug counselor.
■ Provide a reason for each ranking.

Less Than Perfect

Chuck rushes his wife, Diane, to the hospital. Her contractions are coming closer and closer together. The day they have been so patiently awaiting has finally arrived—the birth of their first child. Despite his nervousness and excitement, Chuck cannot think of a happier moment in his life.

After the birth, the obstetrics nurse tells Chuck and Diane that their baby girl has a genetic defect that is not correctable. She has visible deformities and moderate-to-severe brain damage. The doctor explains that their baby might live, but she most definitely will not live a normal life. After outlining the expensive medical care required, the doctor suggests that they allow the infant to die. If they agree, the hospital's normal procedure would be to discontinue medical care and feeding of the infant.

At first Diane disagrees, but Chuck insists that they follow the doctor's advice. Reluctantly, she goes along with Chuck's decision. The doctor places the order on the baby's medical chart. The obstetrics nurse sees the doctor's orders and strongly disagrees. She feels that the doctor is murdering an innocent, helpless child. The nurse is quietly taken off the case. The baby dies two days later.

■ Rank the decisions of the following characters from best to worst: Chuck, Diane, the doctor, the obstetrics nurse.
■ Provide a reason for each ranking.

Partying

"Of course there will be alcohol, Pam. It's going to be a party," Jeff laughs as he hands Pam the map and leaves for class.

Pam closes her locker and heads for class. "Why does partying always have to include drinking?" she wonders. She thinks she probably will go because everyone she knows will be there. "It'll be all right, since I don't drink," she muses. "Besides, the last party was fun. Jerri was there, and she acted so funny when she was drunk."

Pam's parents don't like her going to parties where there is alcohol. Pam resolves not to lie to them, but she doesn't plan to volunteer any information either.

When Pam gets home that afternoon, she finds a postcard from Saint Aggie's reminding her of the upcoming youth group social, which is the same night as Jeff's party. Pam is sure her parents will pressure her into attending the church social. Sure enough, the day of the party, Pam's parents ask her what time she will be home from the church social. She tells them she isn't in the mood for church activities and prefers to go out with her girlfriends. Her parents reluctantly agree. Pam goes to the party with her girlfriends. She rationalizes that maybe she can keep them from getting too drunk.

- Rank the actions and the decisions of the following characters from best to worst: Jeff, Pam, Jerri, Pam's parents, Pam's girlfriends.
- Provide a reason for each ranking.

X-Rated

Kurt cannot believe his eyes. Right in the middle of the living room, *his* living room, is an X-rated movie on the television. "Hey, Kurt," says Mike, his older brother, "me and the guys are putting the new VCR to good use while Mom's at work." Several of Mike's friends are scattered around the room. Mike smirks. "Oh, come on, Kurt, don't look at me like that. Jack here enlisted in the navy, and we figured this would be a good send-off party for him." Jack, who is sprawled across the couch, grins. "Hey, it's only a movie," Mike continues. "It's no big deal. Mom will never find out if you don't tell her. So why don't you get lost for the afternoon."

As Kurt leaves the house, he can hear Mike and his friends laughing. He is ready to give up on his brother. He is a hopeless case. Mike used to go to Mass and youth group meetings. He had even been president of the youth group once. But something has happened to Mike, and Kurt doesn't know what.

The next day, Mike apologizes to Kurt and asks him again not to tell their mother. He promises that it won't happen again. "Sure," Kurt thinks. "I've heard that before." He walks out of the room.

- Rank the following characters from best to worst: Kurt, Mike, Mike's friends, Jack.
- Provide a reason for each ranking.

The Diary

Michelle's mother finds Michelle's diary accidentally while she is cleaning her closet. She knows she shouldn't read it, but her curiosity gets the better of her, and the next thing she knows she is reading her daughter's diary.

She is stunned. She cannot believe that her daughter is capable of such anger toward her parents. She has always thought that she and her daughter have a great relationship, but the things her daughter wrote about her after some of their arguments shock her. She had no idea her daughter had ever had anything to drink, let alone been drunk. And the things Michelle said about her dates startle her. She wonders if kids really do things like that nowadays. The language also puts her off. She had no idea her daughter had ever used any swear words, let alone the one she so freely used in her diary.

She shows Michelle's diary to her husband. He is upset with his wife for reading the diary. He is also shocked at what is in it. He can't bring himself to read it, but his wife told him enough. Even though he believes that Michelle's privacy has been violated, he also believes that something needs to be done about Michelle.

Michelle's parents decide to confront their daughter. Michelle completely falls apart. She can't believe that her own parents would violate her privacy and read her diary. The argument becomes so heated and ugly that Michelle leaves and goes to stay with a friend. Her parents have no idea where she has gone, but neither of them feel the least regret for what they did; the fact that Michelle ran away only confirms that they did the right thing. Michelle knows she is wrong, they reason, and that is why she ran away.

■ Rank the actions and the decisions of the following characters best to worst: Michelle, Michelle's mother, Michelle's father.

■ Provide a reason for each ranking.

Secret Birth Control

Robin sleeps with her boyfriend, but that isn't "sleeping around," she thinks. She hopes that someday they will get married. Although Seth isn't the only boyfriend she has slept with, Robin feels that people who love each other should have sex together; it is part of love.

Robin feels that as an eighteen-year-old and a senior, she is old enough to make her own decisions. She decides it is the right time to have a frank discussion with her mom. Robin tells her mom that she thinks it is okay to have sex with someone you love and that, in fact, she has been having sex with Seth. She also tells her mother that she thinks abortion is wrong and that she wants to use birth control pills. Her mother is appalled at the whole conversation and refuses to even discuss the possibility of birth control. She orders Robin to break up with Seth and not to have sex with anyone. Robin reminds her mother that she can obtain birth control pills without her permission. Her mother threatens to destroy any birth control pills or devices she finds.

Robin continues having sex with Seth and gets birth control pills at the local clinic. A couple of months later, Robin's mother finds the pills and throws them away. Robin is so angry that she continues to have sex with Seth without any protection, and two months later she discovers she is pregnant. Because she doesn't believe in abortion, she tells Seth that she is pregnant, fully expecting him to agree to get married. Seth says that he has no intention of getting married and blames her for getting pregnant in the first place.

Robin breaks up with Seth and has an abortion. All her parents know is that she has broken up with Seth. They are proud of Robin and glad to see that she has responded to their wishes.

- Rank the decisions of the following characters from best to worst: Robin, Seth, Robin's mom.
- Provide a reason for each ranking.

The End of a Future

The "animals." That's what everyone at school calls them. Barry, Brad, Aaron, Jim, and Ken are all seniors. Their contribution to the football team is vital if the team is to win the conference championship, which everyone expects, even though the season is just beginning.

Barry has a 3.8 grade point average and is already being recruited by prestigious colleges. His parents are unemployed, but Barry is looking forward to a full scholarship.

Although Brad is considered one of the "animals," he is a lot different from the rest of them. He doesn't drink or party. Brad has the respect of all the other guys.

The Tuesday night before the season opener, the "animals" decide to have a secret drinking party to celebrate the beginning of a great season. They need Brad's presence for an alibi. Their parents trust Brad, and if they say they are going to Brad's, no questions will be asked. Brad doesn't like the idea, but he says he will go along with it as long as the guys agree to let him drive. They say no. They have too much respect for Brad to want him around while they get drunk. Brad agrees to cover for them, but he doesn't like it.

On the way home from the party, Barry's car is pulled over by the police. All the guys are hauled down to the police station, and their parents are called. The football coach hears about it the next day and angrily drops all the "animals" from the team. Barry feels that his future is ruined. He becomes so depressed that he begins drinking every weekend. His grades fall, and eventually he drops out of school and becomes an alcoholic.

Brad goes on to college, but he is never the same. He blames himself for Barry's disastrous one-night drinking binge. He drops out of church and becomes a real loner.

- Rank the actions and the decisions of the following characters from best to worst: Barry, Brad, the football coach.
- Provide a reason for each ranking.

The Quitter?

Bob, a high school senior, receives a car for his eighteenth birthday. His parents tell him he will have to pay for the gas and insurance himself. They feel he can handle this because he has been working at a fast-food restaurant for almost a year. If not for that, they wouldn't be able to afford the car.

What they don't know is that Bob hates his job. He is making minimum wage, and his bosses are treating him badly—making him do all the jobs that the higher-paid employees don't want to do. He is always at the bottom of the totem pole when it comes to scheduling, as well. They often schedule him to work Friday and Saturday nights. And then when he shows up, they tell him that they need him for only an hour or that they don't need him at all. When work is extra busy, they make him stay late to close the restaurant because the higher-paid employees have plans. Bob has been planning to quit for a long time. Of course, he is excited about the car, but he also wants to quit his job.

After he has had the car a month, he tells his parents that he wants to quit work. Bob explains that he is being mistreated at work and that his bosses refuse to listen to his complaints. But his parents insist that they bought the car with the expectation that Bob would pay for its upkeep. "It's too late," Bob shrugs. "I already gave notice." His father angrily calls Bob's boss, who tells him that Bob would have been fired for his terrible attitude and his laziness.

Bob's dad accuses Bob of being irresponsible, lazy, selfish, and dishonest because he misled his parents until after they bought the car. Bob's dad threatens to sell the car if Bob loses his job.

Bob, devastated, insists that his boss isn't telling the truth. "I'm not lazy," he tells his father. "I just don't like being treated like a slave. I worked six months longer than I wanted to, just to prove that I'm not lazy or irresponsible."

His parents refuse to accept his explanation. They remind him that many people work at jobs that they don't like and that people have to do what they don't want to.

"I understand all that," Bob says. "But sometimes you have to stand up to people who mistreat you. I don't want to ignore my responsibilities; I just want to be treated like a human being."

His parents give him an ultimatum: Work or no car. Bob holds to his decision to quit his job. His parents sell the car.

- Rank the actions and the decisions of the following characters in this story from best to worst: Bob, Bob's parents, Bob's boss.
- Provide a reason for each ranking.

Fatso

Jenay, a junior in high school, is basically a happy girl. Everything is going great until the end of her junior year, and then the bottom falls out. Not only do her parents divorce, but her mother remarries almost immediately. Everyone at school knows about the divorce and knows that Jenay's mom was involved with another guy before the divorce. Jenay doesn't get along well with her father, but she hates Gary, her new stepfather. She understands why her mother wanted to get a divorce, but since her mother met Gary, she has had no time for Jenay; all she thinks about is him. Jenay feels that she is in the way, and when she asks her mother about it, her mother simply says that Jenay is overreacting and not being understanding.

Jenay thinks about going to live with her father but decides against it for a number of reasons. First, she doesn't get along with him, although she does feel sorry for him because her mom had been unfaithful. And second, Jenay's mother made it clear that if Jenay goes with her father, it would be considered a betrayal.

Jenay is depressed a lot. She quickly discovers that eating helps. She doesn't notice it at first, but slowly, gradually, she realizes that she is eating all the time and gaining weight, lots of weight. The more weight she gains, the more Jenay's mom complains. She sometimes threatens to send Jenay to her father's if she doesn't stop overeating. In fact, Jenay calls her father and asks whether she can live with him. He says he has his own life to live.

Jenay has been going steady with Martin for almost two years, and she is relieved that he still cares for her despite her weight problem. They have been sexually active almost from the beginning. Then the worst happens: Jenay finds a note that he wrote to a friend. It says:

Bob, I've got to figure out how to dump Jenay, quick. I've wanted to get rid of Fatso for a long time, but I didn't want to hurt her feelings and, besides, the sex is great.

The next day Jenay swallows a whole bottle of sleeping pills.

- Rank the actions of the following characters from best to worst: Jenay, Martin, Jenay's mother, Jenay's father, Jenay's stepfather.
- Provide a reason for each ranking.

The Adulterer

Once upon a time, there lived a couple who had been married several years. The husband, Harry, was a traveling salesman who had to be away from home a great deal, often as much as twelve to fifteen hours a day. The salesman's wife, Jean, spent many lonely hours at home. One night, they found time to attend a cocktail party at which another man, a widower who lived across the river, became friendly with Jean and began seeing her regularly. She was flattered and gradually found herself falling in love with him. She would journey across the river (via the bridge) several times a week to visit the widower at his house, where they would secretly make love. Because her husband was jealous, Jean was careful to return home by six in the evening, which was when her husband either comes home for dinner or phones in. Thus, he never knew that Jean was seeing the widower, and the marriage was preserved.

One day, while Jean was at the widower's house, a sniper climbed the bridge and began shooting at people crossing the bridge. The police blocked the bridge and would let no one cross. When Jean tried to return home, she found that she could not cross the bridge due to the sniper. She went instead to the ferryboat, which was the only other way across the river. When she tried to board the ferry, she found she had no money and could not pay the toll. The ferryboat driver refused her passage, despite much begging and pleading on her part. Time was running short. She thought of a friend who lived near the ferryboat dock who might possibly lend her the money needed to cross the river. Jean's friend, however, refused to lend her the money because she was aware of Jean's conduct with the widower. She felt that it would be immoral for her to lend the money, helping Jean to continue her relationship with her lover. Now Jean was getting panicky, knowing that Harry would soon return home and discover that she was gone, so she decided to take her chances on the bridge. She drove through the police barricade and sped across the bridge despite warnings and orders to halt. The sniper carefully took aim and shot Jean as she tried to cross. Her car plunged into the river below. She was killed instantly.

■ Who was most responsible for Jean's death? Rank the characters from most responsible to least responsible: Harry, Jean, Jean's lover, the sniper, the ferryboat operator, the friend, anyone else (e.g., the police or society).

■ Provide a reason for each ranking.

PART 4
Giving Advice

Introduction

This section asks the young people to assume the role of an advice-giver. This "Ann Landers" procedure functions as an interesting and fun occasion for the young people to review their own opinions. This strategy works best when it avoids facile solutions and moves the participants to ask: Why would I give this advice? If I were this person, would I be willing or able to do this? Am I willing to walk with this person as he or she follows *my* advice? If the young people cannot answer the last two questions in the affirmative, suggest that perhaps they consider rethinking their advice.

Violent Dilemma

Susan is totally confused. She has known for a long time that her father physically abuses her mother, but she feels helpless to do anything. Susan's mother absolutely refuses to talk about it and doesn't allow Susan to tell anyone. She says "I love your father, and if you tell, your father might end up in jail." Susan doesn't want her father to go to jail, nor does she want to cause her mother any more pain.

But last night was too much. Her father not only beat her mother severely but also tried to hurt Susan. She ran out of the house and came to you. She wants to know what to do.

- What are Susan's options?
- What would you advise her to do? Why?

Christmas in Hawaii

Paula's parents have been divorced for five years now. Her father has remarried and lives out of the area. Paula lives with her mother and sees her father once or twice a year. Paula has been invited to go to Hawaii with her father and stepmother during Christmas break. Paula's mother tells her that she doesn't want to spend Christmas alone. All Paula knows is that she loves her mother *and* her father and wouldn't want to hurt either of them. She comes to you for advice.

- What are Paula's options?
- What would you advise her to do? Why?

Big Sister, Big Problem

Belinda is fifteen and her sister, Teresa, who is severely mentally retarded, is twenty-one. Because Belinda's parents both work, she takes care of Teresa a lot. Belinda knows she shouldn't feel resentment, but she does. She wishes her parents would put Teresa in a special home, but they say that they don't have enough money. Teresa's behavior embarrasses Belinda and her friends. Belinda knows that that is why her friends don't like to come over anymore. In fact, Belinda sometimes feels like her friends wonder about *her*. Belinda is beginning to hate Teresa. She knows that she needs to do something. She comes to you for help.

- What are Belinda's options?
- What would you advise her to do? Why?

Family Ties

Ricardo's family has seen noticeable changes in his life since he got involved with the youth group at church. His grades are beginning to improve. Overall, the improvement is great—except for one problem.

Ricardo's family has always spent a great deal of time together. But now that Ricardo is involved in the church, he is gone all the time—Sunday morning, Sunday night, Wednesday night, and almost every weekend—at some church activity.

Ricardo's parents tell him that they mind his being gone so much. They feel that he has become a stranger in the house and that he is losing touch with his brothers and sisters. They tell him that he has to cut back on church activities and stay home during school nights.

Ricardo is crushed. He feels that if he quits going, he will be right back where he was a few months ago—hanging around with the wrong crowd and goofing off in school. He comes to you for help.

- What are Ricardo's options?
- What would you advise him to do? Why?

Would God Play the Lottery?

Some dads fish, some dads hunt, but Gary's dad gambles. For as long as Gary can remember, his dad has taken his family to the horse races in the summer and to Las Vegas in the winter. Most of the time his dad would lose—only up to a certain amount, and then he would quit. But every once in awhile he would win, and those were wonderful times. Gary's dad would take the whole family out to dinner, and there would be a big family celebration with surprise gifts for everyone.

A week ago, Gary was invited to a friend's church to hear a guest speaker talk about the dangers of gambling. It had never occurred to Gary that gambling might be wrong. Gary knew some people become addicted to gambling, and he understood how it could be wrong for some people—but this speaker was saying that *no* Christian should gamble. Gary is confused. He comes to you for advice.

- What are Gary's options?
- What would you advise him to do? Why?

Older Man, Younger Woman

Melissa is a ninth grader at San Anselmo High School. She's fifteen but looks much older. Her mother has made it clear that Melissa cannot date senior guys, and that has never been a problem—until now. Melissa thinks that Gordie is a total babe. He is active in the church youth group and is a great guy.

Melissa isn't the type to sneak around. She and her mom have a good relationship, and she feels sure that her mom will understand. So Melissa asks her mom if she can go out with Gordie, but the answer is no.

Melissa tries to change her mom's mind, but she won't listen to reason. Melissa wants to do what her mom says, and she doesn't want to damage their relationship, but she *doesn't* want to lose Gordie. She comes to you for help.

- What are Melissa's options?
- What would you advise her to do? Why?

Who to Tell?

Fifteen months ago Denise had an abortion. It was an emotionally horrifying experience that took Denise almost a year of counseling to get over. Denise now feels that abortion is wrong and believes that God has forgiven her. She has been trying to get on with her life.

For the past few months, Denise has been getting pretty serious with a new guy, Graham. They have had some wonderful talks about a lot of issues, including abortion. Graham made it clear that he thinks abortion is wrong—he even hates the thought of it.

Denise is miserable because the more serious she gets with Graham, the more she feels the need to tell him what she has done. She thinks that he might find out anyway because her old boyfriend knows, and her best girlfriend knows. Even though they have been sworn to secrecy, Denise knows that the truth about her might slip out. Denise comes to you for advice.

- What are Denise's options?
- What would you advise her to do? Why?

Good Friend to a Bad Friend

Samantha and Crista have been good friends for a long time. But over the last year, Samantha has dropped out of church, started working at a fast-food place, bought a car, and taken up smoking. She has also been drinking quite a bit at parties. She is still the bubbly, fun person she always was. She says that she has outgrown the church and all that religion stuff, but she doesn't see that anything else has changed.

Samantha's parents are concerned and ask Crista to stick with Samantha and try to help her. However, Crista's parents insist that they don't want her hanging around Samantha anymore because they think Samantha is a bad influence. Crista admits to herself that Samantha has influenced her negatively lately, but she doesn't see this as a big problem. Crista doesn't know what to do. She wants to be Samantha's friend, but her parents say absolutely not. Crista comes to you for advice.

- What are Crista's options?
- What would you advise her to do? Why?

The Boy Who Wouldn't Give Up

Jill and Gordon have been going together for three years. From the beginning, Jill has known that the relationship has problems, but she keeps thinking that either they will break up or things will get better. But things aren't getting better, nor are Gordon and Jill breaking up. Gordon becomes more and more possessive and demanding. Finally, when Jill graduates from high school, she tells Gordon it is over. Gordon is blown away—he had thought that they were getting married. He cries, pleads, and becomes angry, but Jill sticks to her decision.

Then Gordon begins calling her at home every night and at work every morning, but Jill refuses to talk to him. He follows her home from work and tries to talk to her. One night Jill hears scratching at her window. It is Gordon. Jill calls her father, and he firmly convinces Gordon that coming around at two o'clock in the morning is not a good idea.

Finally, Jill gets a letter from Gordon. He writes that if she doesn't come back to him, he will seriously consider killing himself. The letter hurts Jill. She certainly doesn't want to be responsible for Gordon taking his life. She comes to you for advice.

- What are Jill's options?
- What would you advise her to do? Why?

Little Sister

Lauren has decided that it is tough being the first child, especially if you are a girl. She feels that her parents tried to keep her from growing up too quickly. Lauren remembers every fight she had with her parents about growing up. They argued about the proper age to begin wearing panty hose and makeup. They argued about getting her ears pierced and then about the size of her earrings. But now her little sister, Leslie, is growing up, and Lauren thinks she gets to do anything she wants. Although Leslie is only twelve, she is already wearing lip gloss, big earrings, and high heels. Lauren thinks she looks like a miniature twenty-year-old. Lauren has brought this up to her parents several times, but they deny that Leslie is getting away with anything. Lauren is resentful and feels cheated. Now her parents are telling her she cannot drive alone until she is eighteen. Lauren blows up at her parents and leaves home. She comes to your house. She wants to know what to do.

- What are Lauren's options?
- What would you advise her to do? Why?

The Wrong Curves

Stacy keeps staring at the mirror. She has known for the last few months that something is wrong, but she hasn't been able to figure out what. Now she knows. There is something very wrong with her back. Her shoulders aren't even, and her back seems to have a slight curve to it. Stacy wants to believe that it is just an illusion, that she is being a hypochondriac—but she cannot deny it anymore.

Stacy tells her parents. They take Stacy to a doctor for an examination. She explains that about 10 percent of all teenagers have some form of scoliosis, or curvature of the spine. She says that if Stacy wears a brace for three years, the scoliosis can be arrested or corrected. However, the doctor says that Stacy would have to wear the brace religiously. Then the doctor shows her the brace. She is stunned. Stacy begins to cry. She knows that she would have to give up the beach, the bikinis, her favorite sports. She figures she would look like a freak for three years. Stacy makes up her mind right then that she would not wear that brace. She secretly feels that God is responsible for her condition and that if she prayed, God could heal her. She comes to you for advice.

- What are Stacy's options?
- What would you advise her to do? Why?

The Loner

Don isn't stupid. He feels that everyone thinks about him in the same way that he thinks about himself. Don thinks he isn't good looking—just plain weird looking. A lot of kids make fun of him. He wishes he could say, "Well, I may be weird looking, but at least I get straight A's" or "Go ahead, don't be friends with me. I'll drive my Porsche by myself." But Don's folks don't have much money and his grades are average. Don is lonely. All he wants is a friend. He doesn't think that that is too much to ask for. You are the only one in class who even acts like he exists, so he comes to you for advice.

- What are Don's options?
- What would you advise him to do? Why?